MYTHS AND LEGENDS OF THE MACKINACS AND THE LAKE REGION

by Grace Franks Kane

Cincinnati, Ohio
1897

Reprinted 1972, 1976, 1986

BLACK LETTER PRESS

SBN No. 0-912382-09-0

I especially want to thank Mary Engen and Orson Grant
for motivating me to republish this book.

Cover art by Robert Nelson

Dedication.

To

My Husband

I dedicate this book,

wishing only that it were better worth

the partial and patient perusal

that I know

He

will give it.

DETROIT, 1897.

CONTENTS.

AUTHOR'S NOTE.

THESE Legends have been gathered from the works of Parkman, Grimm, Tanner, Van Fleet, and other writers, some of whose very names have been forgotten, and from many other sources, but *especially* from the word-of-mouth tales of the Indians of the Lake Region and their half-breed descendants, among whom the greater part of my life was spent.

The spelling and pronunciation of Indian names and words have always been difficult. I give them, as nearly as possible, as they sound, to simplify them for the reader.

It was at the suggestion of ex-Senator T. W. Ferry, of Michigan, who was born at the Mission House in Mackinac, that these fragments of a dying race were collected and published.

GRACE FRANKS KANE.

DETROIT, 1897

THE FAIRY ISLE.

Bright Island in the midst of Northern Seas,
  How light thou rid'st upon the wave!
Yet none may know thy beauteous ease,
  Nor in thy golden sunshine lave,
With such pure joy as once belonged
To those great warriors who thronged
To worship on thy shores;—to seek,
Within thy heart, enchanted paths, thick
And impenetrable and dark, yet
Cool with leaves of interwoven branches met—
Place for their sacred dead—
In time long sped.

No eye can see its brightness as they saw.
  A golden mist enshrouded that fair isle!
No stranger foot had e'er transgressed the law
  Made by the worship of their gods erstwhile—
The thousand thousand gods who smile,
Or gods whose voice of thunder did beguile
The storm-tossed sailor of past histories
To seek its shelter, solve its mysteries,
And die upon its shore—
Be seen no more.

The waking fancy of an ancient dream
  Pervades the thought, and thrills the heart
And mind of one whose children seem
  By native right a living part
Of that long past, which once had been
Their heritage and boast, now lost to them.
Call it the "fancy of a dream,"
To paint the longing of a heart—
To give those reverend children of the wood
The ancient Turtle-fields—the jewels of the good!
What bliss for them, to rest at will,
Sweet Fairy Isle, upon thy terraced hill.

THE MISSION HOUSE.

Myths and Legends of the Mackinacs

AND THE

Lake Region.

LEGEND OF ARCHED ROCK.

IT is said that the Island of Mackinac is cavernous, and that its subterranean grottoes, halls, and passages, known only to the Indians, were used as burial places for their dead. These underground paths run in various directions, connecting the many islands of the straits with the mainland.

The picturesque span known as the Arched Rock is all that remains of the grand portal or entrance to the subterranean sleeping-place of departed souls. The covering of this magnificent gateway, Father Time, with his slow-working fingers, destroyed ages ago. Tradition tells us that this happened suddenly: a collapse of the earth, leaving the arch as it is, with which Time is still slowly busy.

Sis-kow-it was a brave warrior. His father was the Morning Sun, whose rose-cloud chariot, driven by winged zephyrs, bore him around the world in a single day. Sis-kow-it loved the Moon's daughter, Ad-dik-keem-maig, whom he often had met while swimming in the waters of the Ka-re-gwon-di (Deep Lake).

The Moon had many children, but Ad-dik-keem-maig was known to be her favorite child. Sis-kow-it knew the Moon Mother to be a cold creature, very distant and proud to those beneath her; but he was a great brave, and had no fear on the score of family. He came of an ancient race—could trace his lineage in an unbroken line since the world began—and it was with a great pride as well as a great love in his heart that he besought of the Moon the hand of her loveliest child.

Before giving her consent to their union, the Moon looked in upon Ai-kie-wai-se (Wise Man Who Had Lived Long Upon the Earth), whose lodge was set in the deep forest near the Cave of Skulls. Being a prophet, he could foretell events, and look into the past as well as the future. Having learned from him that Sis-kow-it was a suitable husband for her daughter, the Moon-Mother joined their hands in betrothal, stipulating only that she should pass twelve times around the earth before Sis-kow-it should take the husband's place in the lodge of Ad-dik-keem-maig.

Happy indeed were the youthful couple, strong in the mutual love which enabled them to endure with patience their term of probation. Evening's soft light often shone upon them as they wandered on the shore of the placid Ka-re-gwon-di, through the paths of the forest or over the dewy hills, enveloped always in the ample folds of the love-blanket which Sis-kow-it had presented to his betrothed. The bright sister-stars stood sentinel, while the pine, the cedar, and the spruce filled the air with delicious perfumes for their delectation, as they clambered over crags and mossy boulders, whispering vows of constancy and planning their "life-walk," until they reached the cliff above the graves of those departed braves of past ages. Mysterious and gruesome was the place of tryst, but the lovers were not afraid, for the stars kept watch as they sat in the shadow.

Months passed, and the Moon, who had nearly completed her round of visits, began to be averse to the contemplated marriage and wished to have it postponed. The gentle Ad-dik-keem-maig had always been an obedient child, but at last there came a time when she felt that she must think and act for herself.

The lovers were about to be parted. The Sun drove up one morning in a chariot of thick clouds, driven by the North Winds, to declare war upon a neighboring nation. The news was scattered in gusts among the people, filling many eyes with tears and every ear with pain and dismay. Especially distressing was the command that Sis-kow-it should lead a band of braves to battle, as it was known that his wedding-day was near at hand and the arrangements for it almost completed. Sadly the youth prepared to obey the order of his chief and to bid farewell to the maiden of his love.

"Fare thee well, then, my beloved. Weep not for me. I shall soon return. Let thy parting smile cheer me—thy courage infuse my heart, and cause the enemy to tremble before the strength which love hath given to my arm. Let thy faith be as strong as thy love! Meet my return with the same virgin smile which thou bendest upon me as I depart. Fear not. I shall vanquish my enemies and return in the garment of victory, which none but brave conquerors wear. Then shall I clasp my wife, who shall ever be fairest upon the earth in the eyes of her husband, and who shall bring a sweetness into his lodge like that of the sweet-briar which grows upon the shoulders of the Great Turtle!"

A light but propitious breeze floated over the bosom of Ka-re-gwon-di, bearing Sis-kow-it and his braves away from the island and from Ad-dik-keem-maig. With a great patience the maiden set herself to await his home-coming. She hoped that her mother, the Moon, would do all her traveling around the world during Sis-kow-it's absence, for then their wedding-day would be at hand.

Her favorite haunt was the cliff above the "Cave of the Dead." Here would she sit and gaze for hours upon the blue waters, her eyes constantly fixed upon the course which the warriors had taken. She often heard the mournful cry of the loon at these times, and her heart grew heavy with dread of the omen. Even on those bright days when Father Sun smiled on the waters, or at night when the shimmering glances of her young sisters, the stars, shone in its placid depths, she was miserable because of the presence of the bird of ill-luck. Once these beauties had been her chief joy, but now she could not shake off the terrible dread which clung to her.

While the maiden was thus employed, she became the object of the longing and impassioned love of Ki-tah-coin-se (Climber), a young Indian of a neighboring tribe, and a would-be suitor. The silent and persistent gaze of the Climber, accompanied by the strains of the musical pi-be gwon, signified his desire to make Ad-dik-keem-maig his wife. She turned from him in refusal, but he continued his ardent demonstrations in the hope that she would change her mind and at least listen to his declaration. The Sun, who witnessed the girl's distress at the fellow's impudence, grew so angry that he plunged into a bank of clouds to quench his wrath, quitting the day an hour earlier than usual because he cared not to look upon the would-be successor of his son, much less countenance such interference in Sis-kow-it's right of possession.

The Moon, herself, could not move the bold wooer, though she was cold enough for anything; so she withdrew for a time, but returned in company with the Night Wind, who tossed the impertinent Climber about until he was forced to throw his music away and seek shelter in the woods. How little the friends of Ad-dik-keem-maig knew the strength and steadfastness of her nature!

The Moon might change, but not this faithful heart.

But one evening when the Winds were still the Climber ventured once more within speaking distance, and upon promise of news of the absent warriors won the girl's instant attention; while the suspicious Moon drew near to hear what was said by the unscrupulous one, in his effort to win her daughter from Sis-kow-it.

"The prophet had said that Sis-kow-it was already in the Place of Souls," repeated Ki-tah-coin-si; and Ad-dik-keem-maig, terrified at the news, instead of turning to him for comfort, as he had hoped she would, made her way with all speed to the lodge of the Aged One, where, with tears in her eyes and a grief fine to see, she begged him to reveal the *truth* in regard to her lover, at the same time repeating the story of Ki-tah-coin-si.

The Aged Man calmed her fears by declaring the Climber to have been deceived by a false prophet—that, "though wounded, by every sign Sis-kow-it had been victorious, and was now on his way home. He would recover from his wounds, but *might* be crippled for life." This last was added to test the maiden's loyalty and love, and the first word she uttered on hearing the revelation of the priest satisfied him of her faithfulness and devotion to her lover.

"All is well, then, since he lives and will return soon! I shall be his wife! *My* feet shall be his feet! *My* shoulders shall bear his burden!" was all Ad-dik-keem-maig found voice to say, though her eyes told all her gratitude to the seer, and this was his best reward.

"What do I hear?" cried the Moon, who had again followed to listen. "Shall *my* daughter—the bright one, the beautiful—she of the truthful eye, whose hair is like the glossy wing of the crow, whose step is as swift as the roe which courses the plains—shall *she* wed with a crooked man? Never! I withdraw my consent. They shall *never* marry!" And the Moon sailed away in search of Ki-tah-coin-si, who, fearing the wrath of the Aged Man, had hidden himself in the underbrush. Half the night was gone when the Moon brought him to light. She bade him fear nothing—that she was his friend and would assist him to marry Ad-dik-keem-maig, even to the carrying of her off by force.

Arrangements were made by them for the immediate consummation of this plan; the approach of the war party having been foretold, they determined that the marriage should be over before they reached the island.

The Sun, informed of the change in the Moon, came upon the scene even more angry than when he had left them the evening before. He made after the pale thing, and chased her till she was out of sight; but he smiled upon Ad-dik-keem-maig, who protested against her mother's cruelty, and vowed that she would wed with none but Sis-kow-it. The Sun promised to assist her to the extent of his power, and forthwith fell upon the

Climber with such fierceness that the fellow, strong and powerful though he was, sunk to the earth and became so ill from the beating given him by the Sun, that the old Moon was put to it to keep him alive at all.

While the Moon was in attendance upon the Climber, the Sun was on his way to meet the returning warriors; and it was only during his absence that the schemers waxed strong enough to complete the arrangements for the proposed abduction and marriage. And vainly did the terrified girl protest against the injustice done her lover.

"O Mother Moon! thou art cruel," she cried. "Be not in such haste to condemn. A little patience, a little time, and we shall see for ourselves if the hurt of Sis-kow-it is beyond help."

But the Moon would not be moved from her course. "To-morrow," she said, "to-morrow thou shalt wed Ki-tah-coin-si." She grew red in the face, though, when she heard the faithful girl's answer.

"I will wed with none but the man I love, whose heart I have, who hath my faith! The Master of life hath joined our hearts; in life, in death, they shall not be divided. There is no other way for me. I did not make myself—I can not yield. I love him—as I know him—well. My dreams are all for him. His hand will I take, and no other. My ears are deaf to thy cruel threatenings! *Torture* my body; *that* would soon be dead, but my spirit shall live! My resolve is taken. The Moon hears?"

Ki-tah-coin-si, warned that the war party would soon arrive, determined to carry out his plans immediately. The small hours after midnight should see the maiden his. No time was to be lost. He hurried away to consult his mother-in-law; but the threatening voice of the angry Manitou set the Moon trembling, and at the last moment she had deserted the Climber, making a sorry figure as she staggered and zigzagged down the misty paths of the milky way in her haste to hide among some thick clouds which were hurrying across the sky.

Poor Ad-dik-keem-maig, knowing nothing of the nearness of Sis-kow-it, and full of forebodings of evil—fearful of everything, doubtful of everything save her own faithfulness—sought once more the trysting-place upon the cliff, there to commune with her own thoughts, and await, with what patience she could, news from her lover.

Her dreams, of late, had been troubled. In them she had seen herself united to her lover; but the conditions of their union were hidden from her, and she longed for the return of Sis-kow-it, that her fears might be set at rest. "The Sun is our friend," she said to herself. "Gitchie Manitou has frightened the Moon, and even the stars are hiding." She smiled at the thought of the poor little stars trembling behind their curtains of clouds, and gained courage and comfort by saying over and over again to herself: "Every hour brings my lover nearer! Every hour brings my lover nearer!"

A bat flew by, sweeping her cheek with its damp wing. "Was it an omen? What evil did it portend?" A terrible fear shook her, and she almost ceased to breathe, when the mournful cry of the loon smote upon her listening ear as if in answer to her thought. Hark! A snapping twig, a stealthy step!

Lofty and lonely the place of tryst—rock-bound and hidden by thick brush and bramble its approaches—and by the lovers ever deemed an impregnable retreat. Why should fear and doubt fill her heart at this moment? Why tremble and grow cold at the fancied sound of a stealthy step! Again!—many steps! Swiftly and silently she prepared to defend herself. Morning was near, but the darkness still lingered to increase her danger. She could distinguish nothing within its midnight shades; yet she *felt* her danger. Suddenly the dawn gathered strength, and all at once some figures were coming toward her. Her heart seemed not to beat. "Oh, where is Sis-kow-it?"

In a moment these figures, springing toward her, are clearly revealed—foremost is Ki-tah-coin-si. Lithe forms of the hunters whom he had enlisted to aid him in carrying off by force the girl whom he had determined to marry at all hazards, were seen dodging the trees or leaping over boulders which came between them and the object of their search. Fleet of foot are they—yet not fleet enough! In a flash the girl divines their intention and decides upon her course. She can but *die!* She *must not* be taken! Her slender foot is on the brink of the abyss—her graceful figure poised for the spring. *Where, where* is Sis-kow-it?

Morning came sadly out of the East, enveloped in mists, which the Sun came up to drive away—but, alas! too late, too late!

The terrified hunters, instantly comprehending the treachery of the Climber, sprang upon him and impaled him alive on the broken limb of a tree.*

Too late, too late, alas!

The leap is taken!

Hark! The tramp of many feet—and Sis-kow-it is among them! Fully recovered from his slight wounds, he bounds lightly across the open with words of greeting upon his lips for the beloved one whom he seeks.

Without a moment's warning the scene is spread before him, and all his joy is ashes. No words—he sees it all! The form of his betrothed flying downward through the awful space—the still quivering body of the impaled Climber—the angry and excited bearing of the young men—and over all the beauty of the spring morning. He began singing his death song.

The gay shawl of the brave and faithful girl so dear to him lay upon the ground at his feet. He gathered this blanket of love slowly to his heart, and gazed once more into the dark shadows beneath the cliff, which had swallowed his bride. The Sun shone sadly for

---

**Blood maple*, which is the first to turn red in the autumn.

a moment, and Sis-kow-it, thus reminded of his father's sympathy, called upon him to witness the death of a brave man; then, folding the bright shawl about him, he leaped from the cliff.

The Thunder muttered, and the Sun, drawing a veil of black clouds across his face, said:

"Well done, my son! Have thy revenge!" And a mighty bolt, hurled by the lightning, crashed upon the cliff and rent it.

Never more shall the sacred dead be laid within the bosom of the Great Turtle! The approaches to those revered and mysterious depths were forever destroyed by the ammunition of heaven, which tore up the earth and filled the entrance with a conglomerate mass of trees, stones, and great boulders, forever impenetrable.

Some fishermen who were raising their nets in the vicinity of the catastrophe declared that they had seen the lovers darting about beneath the water. The brains of the lovers were transformed into the *white fish* and the *trout*, but "from the brains of the woman were evolved the choicest morsels;" and the magnificent Arch is left as a reminder of the fact.

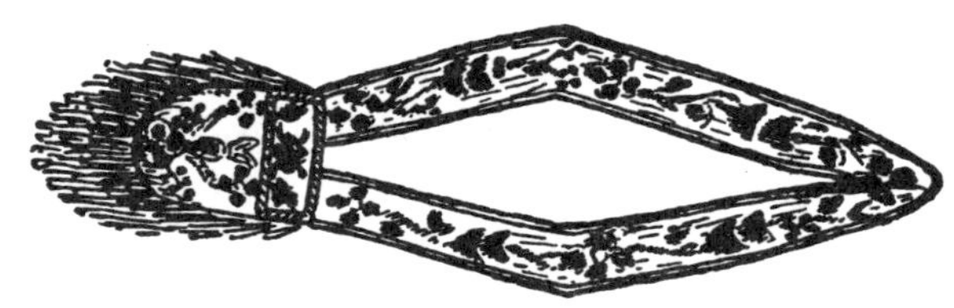

ROBERTSON'S FOLLY.

WHEN the Island of Mackinac was in possession of the British, its garrison had for one of its officers a man by the name of Robertson. He became deeply enamored of a young and beautiful Indian girl, the daughter of a great chief, and the pride of her tribe; and he determined to marry her, though he knew her to be already betrothed to a young warrior of a neighboring tribe; for he also knew that the thought of a life to be spent with the young warrior was odious and revolting to her, compared to a life by the side of the white man (himself) for whom she had confessed her love.

He selected for their home a point of land at the east end of the Island, which overhung the water, and was only accessible from the north side. Knowing the treacherous traits of the Indians, he intended that this side of their retreat should be well guarded, and made secure against intrusion.

Happily married, the young couple repaired to this charming and secluded place, where no prying eyes could invade their privacy. He desired to keep the marriage secret because he feared the vengeance of her people upon his young wife, since she had deserted them for his sake.

Their days of happy idleness, sweet toil, which none but first love and fervent youth enjoys, were of short duration; for, in spite of every precaution against surprise, the enraged lover tracked them to the home made holy by their wedded bliss, and one evening, when he knew the young husband to be on duty at the Fort, stealthily made his way to the spot.

The sun had not yet gone down, but the place was so hedged in with a dense growth of woods and underbrush that candles were required in the house at an early hour; and a light of welcome to the absent husband, when he should be returning, burned at the casement. A beacon of love the discarded lover knew it to be. Peering within the partly opened blind, the savage saw the young wife reclining on a couch, a softly expectant look in her eyes, as the hour of her husband's return drew near. He knew that he must work quickly. With a muttered curse, he raised his hands for one moment toward the setting sun—one moment silent, as if to give the recording Manitou time to note the whispered vow—then, softly turning, stole to the door. No guard in sight! He stepped within, and stood before her. The heroic girl made no sound, no gesture of fear, nor plea for mercy; but she knew that her last hour had come.

He killed her with a swift blow of the knife which he had worn at his belt. His revenge thus secured, he again raised his clasped hands toward the sun, which was now low in the west, spurned with his naked foot the quivering heap of dead loveliness, which had fallen to the floor, and turned to fly.

At this moment Robertson returned. He saw the gesture and the blood, and knew at once what had happened. Upon the ground lay the lifeless body of his young wife, and careless of everything but revenge, he sprang upon her murderer. A fearful struggle ensued. Unconsciously they neared the edge of the cliff; a step, and they were over it, grasping wildly at the empty air, while their voices mingled in a fearful shriek of agony. Down, down they dashed, to fall a mangled heap upon the rocks below.

Suddenly an inky darkness covered the sky, and a storm descended with such violence that the earth shook and trembled as with an earthquake. The Indians took it as a warning from Michibou, their god, that they must no longer expect aid from the Spirit of the Great Turtle; and they sought it elsewhere from that day.

The morning, calm and still after the night of storm, looked upon a frightful scene. The home in ruins, the maiden dead, the mangled corpses of the savage and the gentleman washed high upon the beach by the waves, and blood upon the face of the rock, which the rains of a hundred years have not washed out! Red stains are to be seen there to-day.

LOVER'S LEAP.

SHOT-A-WAY-WAY was a great chief. Shot-a-way-way owned much land. Shot-a-way-way was a great warrior, and painted his face with colors becoming to his station and blood, which descended through a long line of ancestral warriors, and made Shot-a-way-way very brave. Shot-a-way-way wore a knife at his belt, and his tomahawk was always in his hand.

Shot-a-way-way was mighty and powerful. Shot-a-way-way was a great ruler, but he could not govern the heart of his young and beautiful daughter Michinimockonong, though he was hard and cruel enough to forbid her union with the youth to whom she had given her heart.

Shot-a-way-way, the mighty chief and cruel father, commanded that Ge-niw-e-gwon, the youth whom Michinimockonong loved, should go upon the warpath, if he wished to prove his courage and his worthiness of the woman so far above him in station.

Shot-a-way-way commanded that he should not only be victorious in battle, but that he must capture the wonderful war-horse of Saugatuk, the leader of the enemy, who, it was said, always slept with the animal bridled to his hand; and must wear the scalp of Saugatuk at his belt when he returned to claim his bride.

Shot-a-way-way was crafty and cruel, and exacted these things because he did not believe they could be accomplished; but, lest by any chance Ge-niw-e-gwon should succeed in these undertakings, he arranged with Mutch-i-ki-wish, a warrior of treacherous disposition, to kill him. As a reward for this deed, Mutch-i-ki-wish was to have Michinimockonong for his wife.

The young girl grieved long and sorely after parting from the lover for whom so perilous a task was set. Before his leaving, it was agreed between them that she should watch and wait for him at their favorite meeting place—the summit of a great rock which rose abruptly from the side of the cliff and overhung the lake.

Michinimockonong was confident that her brave Ge-niw-e-gwon would return wearing the feathers of victory, for the band of young braves who accompanied him were eager to prove their own worthiness to carry arms, and while fighting for Ge-niw-e-gwon, win laurels for themselves. But Shot-a-way-way, the mighty ruler and chief, was equally confident that Ge-niw-e-gwon would fail.

Her heart all untroubled by suspicions of foul play, Michinimockonong sat each day upon the moss-grown summit of the rock, fashioning her wedding garments. The small moccasins were made from the softest of deer-skin, and embroidered with the brilliantly dyed hairs of the moose—every hair binding a loving thought for the lover for whom she would wear them; the fringes of the dainty leggings were hung with trembling love, the belt of sacred beads which was to girdle her waist was interwoven with it; the gold beads, the silver and copper threads, and each grotesque or brilliant ornament of the various metals with which she decorated the dress shone and reflected the strong and pure passion of her faithful and expectant heart.

Though so well employed, Michinimockonong found the time drag heavily. Her dreams became troubled, and her tender heart ached with dread and foreboding. Strange birds constantly hovered near her, and though well versed in their language, it was long before her well-trained ear and bright intellect could make out the meaning of their songs.

Kenu, the bird of war, sang loudly of glorious victories; the bird of thunder and war rolled forth a song of triumph; a snake bird hummed and hissed of deeds of treachery and darkness; one sang of the conquering Ge-niw-e-gwon's homeward tramp with the scalp of Saugatuk hanging at his belt, while the wild horse of the dead enemy followed tamely the scent of his master's reeking locks; but the sweetest of all the songsters was the Hope bird, which sang and so filled the heart of the loving girl that the woeful words of Pauguk, the Death bird, found no echo there.

A lark, whom she loved because it held the waiting soul of a little brother—dead long years ago—warned her of the treachery of her father toward Ge-niw-e-gwon, and of his intention to wed her to Mutch-i-ki-wish upon his return. The poor girl resumed her seat upon the edge of the cliff, and sang a song so melancholy that the proud heart of Shot-a-way-way was touched, and he sent some women to urge her to leave the dangerous place, promising to be reconciled to Ge-niw-e-gwon on his return if she would join in the dance of welcome to the home-coming warriors. But Michinimockonong no longer trusted her father's promises, for the birds had warned her that they were but snares to entrap her into a marriage with Mutch-i-ki-wish, and forever part her from her lover.

The war birds and the birds of victory, with all the other mysterious songsters save Pauguk, who still sang of death, and the bird of hope, to whose tender and melodious voice Michinimockonong lent a most willing ear, flew away. She would not believe that Ge-niw-e-gwon had gone to the Place of Souls, though a thousand Pauguks foretold it. A loon circled out of the bank of wet clouds, which the sun was fast dispersing, making its plaintive and ominous cry; the flap, flap of its dripping wings reminding her of the paddle blades of the warriors for whom she waited. She sang:

"I thought I saw a loon fly past—
O loon! dread bird for me!
But no; it is my lover's mast,
With snowy sails all taut and fast—
My lover's boat I see.
His paddle in the waves' bright gleam
Flung thousand jewels in my dream,
Which, reaching forth to bind or clasp,
I found were slipping from my grasp.
O loon! dread bird for me!

Thy plumage white, thy call so light,
O loon! dread bird for me!
I thought it told me how he sped
Through seas of blood, o'er heaps of dead,
With scalps of victory!
The story of his triumph heard
In every cry of thine, dread bird!
But shadows gather and grow dark;
I can not see my lover's barque—
The loon's cry mocketh me!
The darkness hides my lover's face;
His face, his form I can not place;
Yet I will haste me to the tryst,
'Gainst which, dread bird, thou'st set thy nest,
O loon! dread bird for me!
And hurl it from its highest place,
To follow faster in the race,
Which sets my spirit free!
My lover's arms await me there—
I seek with joy their tender care.
Ge-niw-e-gwon, my lover, waves
Farewell, dread bird, to thee!
The murmuring waves hide yawning graves!
One leap! my parting spirit leaves
Its vengeance, bird, to thee!"

The sound of her weird singing still floated on the air, as the canoes of the returning warriors drifted through the fog into sight, their paddles and drums keeping time to a song of victory, which mingled and blended in unison with Pauguk's song of death.

She hastened to her lodge, from which at this time even the old women and pappooses were absent. Donning her embroidered wedding dress, she took a quiver of flint-tipped arrows, and with a bow all strung and ready for immediate use, as a suitable gift for the warrior lover whom she still, in spite of warnings, hoped to welcome, hurried again to the place of tryst, to listen for the sound of Ge-niw-e-gwon's well-beloved footstep, and to give him the word of love he hoped for when he came. Far our over the edge of the crumbling rock she leaned to catch the first sight of his gleaming feathers; but she saw instead his dead body, lying all lifeless and cold in a great canoe which was being paddled to the shore by Mutch-i-ki-wish, who thus signified to Shot-a-way-way that he had carried out his part of the contract, and desired prompt payment.

Ge-niw-e-gwon, the dear one for whom she had waited so patiently, was dead. Michinimockonong's brain reeled at the thought. And there, in the same canoe which held his dear remains, sat Mutch-i-ki-wish—as if fearing to lose sight of his victim for a moment—waving his war-bonnet to attract her attention to the freight he carried. With a cry of rage the frenzied girl leaped to the edge of the rock, raised the great bow to her shoulder, and taking unerring aim, sent the lightning-tipped arrow straight through the traitor's heart.

By Mutch-i-ki-wish's backward plunge into the water, the canoe was overturned; and as his enemy sank forever from the sight of men, Ge-niw-e-gwon floated gently into the view of the maiden who had loved him so well.

"He waits for me!" she cried; and turning to the women whom her father had sent to bid her come to the beach, said: "Tell my father *I will not come*. Tell him that Gitchie-Manitou hath said: 'Every man of Shot-away-way's line shall die by fire. Shot-a-way-way, his sons, and his sons' sons shall burn to death in the lodge of the woman they love!'"

With the great bow still in her hand, she turned her eyes upon the broad bosom of the lake, where her beloved still waited. The music of her death song floated upon the air, and before those who listened could prevent, she leaped into the abyss.

Mutch-i-ki-wish knew no resurrection; his body went to the bottom like a stone; but the reunited lovers were seen to join hands and swim away to the Blessed Channels, where they became the father and mother of all fishes.

SKULLS CAVE.

KENU (Thunder Bird) sat within the Cave of Skulls waiting for the Great Spirit, whom he had invoked, to answer his prayer. From the Red Clay Hill he had brought the superior pipe-making material which lay in a heap near the middle of the cave, out of which he intended to fashion pipes for his people, and which were to serve especially as peace-pipes for the women, who were of such contentious disposition and temper as never to be without quarreling.

In his youth Kenu had been famous as a worker in clay, but since he had become a chief, the work had been left to others, as less important than that which devolved upon him as head man of his tribe. Of late the cares of government began to wear upon him; the nice questions he found himself called upon to pronounce and decide, the quarrels he was required to settle, showed him plainly that he was powerless without the aid of Michibou. He brought offerings of sacrifice, made long fasts, imposed penances upon himself which, to one less earnest in his desire for the welfare of his people, would have been unendurable. He had consulted the prophets and medicine men in regard to his troubles, and they had answered him with the exclamation, "Peace! Peace!" He thought they were sending him away unaided, but as "peace" was what he most desired, he determined upon attaining it if possible, and prepared to make the calumets, which, with the Spirit's aid, should bring tranquillity to his nation.

Michibou, the Spirit whom Kenu invoked to aid him, had his home in the caverns of the Great Turtle, and it was only in the "Place of Sacred Things" that his voice could be heard; and to that place Kenu went to "clear his ear" of the noises of the wranglers, lest they should prevent his hearing the Manitou when it should indicate that his petition was to be answered.

Thunder Bird was a great warrior, and it was not by fighting with *women* that he had won fame as such; but though a man and a brave, he owned to a reverent fear of the unearthly powers which lay hidden in the heaps of bones and grinning skulls of dead and gone warriors lying behind him in the Cave; but he feared his contentious women more than he feared the spirits of the dead. He was, himself, possessed of magical powers, by which he could call to his aid the spirits of the earth or air, but of not one of these did his women stand in awe; and so it was that Thunder Bird turned for help to the Ruler of all spirits, with the prayer that the soft clay, out of which he was to fashion the pipes, might be imbued with the *real* spirit of *peace;* and that wherever smoke from them arose should dwell the feeling of brotherhood and love.

Reverently he bent above the hollow place in which were concealed the "Sacred Things" of the tribe, for it was from this place that the voice of the Spirit would come; and as he leaned and waited for the voice, he made with his fingers in the sand along the basin's edge, shapes and designs for the molding of the pipe bowls, if Michibou did not forbid. While thus employed, he was startled to see one of the skeletons roll toward the basin and begin speaking:

"Beneath thy feet find pliant silver." The voice sounded hollow and cold as it came from between the rattling jaws. "Out of it make a tube *a pipe's length*, and in its side a small hole, which shall be for a '*peace note;*' with a covering of clay conceal the reed and place it to dry in the sand which thou hast prepared; with thumb and finger turn the bowl to the shape of thy thought, that thy people may comfort themselves."

Kenu took this as answer to his prayers, and set to work to carry out the instructions he had received, satisfied that his troubles were now over. Silver was found, as indicated by the Skeleton, out of which he formed the pipe stems with a single note, and covered them with wet clay. When dry, the Skeleton took them and blew into each a single note of great sweetness and power, repeating it on each tube successively till the sound was reproduced exactly. Kenu turned the bowls between thumb and finger, joined them to the stems, and placed them between the teeth of the skulls for a trial smoke. This act of courtesy the Skeletons rewarded by adding to the pipes a drawing power which, in the after time, pipe-makers of other nations attempted to imitate, but were never successful in doing; and when Thunder Bird gave the pipes to his people, he did so in the belief that peace would dwell forever among them.

The Skeletons all became living men, and joined the tribe of which Kenu was chief, to become his most valiant warriors. They took wives from among the women, who were no longer quarrelsome; for, with the use of the peace pipe, all disturbances ceased, and they soon were known as the " Peace Makers."

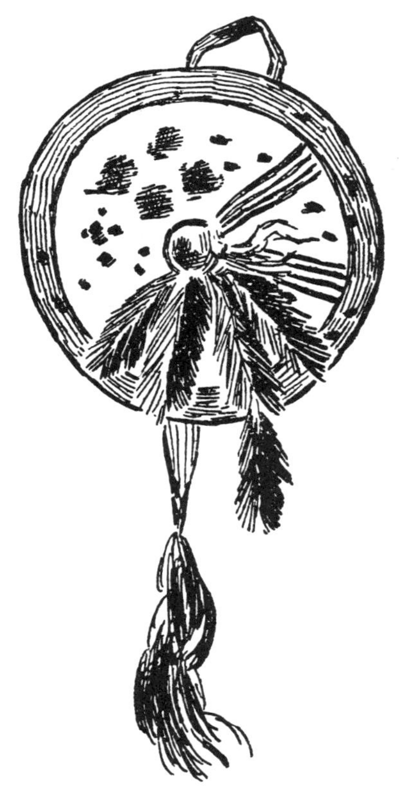

LEGEND OF A CAVE.

IT has been told that the Island of Mackinac is cavernous, and it is believed by many that only by submarine entrances can these underground passages be reached.

One day, when swimming in the lake, the young hunter Nishishshin discovered an opening and explored the caves; but he wisely, as it afterward proved, kept the knowledge of their existence to himself.

Nishishshin loved the daughter of a tyrannical old chief, Pequodenong, who was hated and feared by all, for the reason that he exacted much unnecessary suffering in the way of manhood tests; and not only the young men who were compelled to endure them, but the whole nation of Ojibways were scheming to bring about the tyrant's death.

But Pequodenong discovered that a scheme was on foot to kill him, and, believing that his daughter was a party to the treachery, he included her in the sentence which exacted the lives of the bravest of his tribe, from which, by the assistance of her lover, she *alone* escaped.

The night before the sentence was to be executed, young Nishishshin stole to the maiden's place of imprisonment, cut the thongs which bound her, and led her to the water's edge near the opening of the cave which he had so fortunately discovered.

The girl, being an expert swimmer, plunged fearlessly after her lover when he flung himself into the waves, to rise hand in hand with him in a glistening cavern, which, when they had climbed upon its shelving floors, they found to be roomy and safe from the incoming waters.

In this retreat Nishishshin left his betrothed, secure from harm and all alarms, and for some months she dwelt there, provided for by him.

When Nishishshin had secured the safety of his beloved, he contrived to remove his parents to a place in the North where the tyrant had no power to harm them, and secretly prepared to follow them with the woman whom he wished to make his wife, and for whom, though he had risked much, he was willing to risk more.

Nishishshin had occasionally shown his young associates some wonders of the magician's art, with which he was familiar, and the young men soon had entire faith in his resources, and believed that he frequently held communication with the Great Spirit; and when Nishishshin informed them that he intended making a journey to the nether world, from whence he would bring a wife to accompany him to his new home, they had not a doubt but he would do so.

"At evening," he said, "I will prove my words;" and at an early hour the friends of the young prophet waited near the shore for his appearance, and it was not long before they perceived him rising from the water with a maiden in his arms.

As the lovers were not near enough for recognition, they escaped unharmed, and the fame of the young prophet was spread far and wide; but not until the old tyrant, who had made so many lives miserable, died, and the young couple returned to the island to once more make their home among its leafy glades and dewy hills, was the truth known.

Nishishshin was revered as a great Medicine Man, whose wife ruled the waters and its creatures. They lived long, and their descendants were many.

DEVIL'S KITCHEN.

AIKIE-WAI-SIE was blind and very old; and when his people took down their wigwams and fire-poles, unearthed their sacred things, and removed with all their possessions to the distant hunting grounds, leaving him behind to die of starvation, he thought it very hard. By accident his granddaughter, Willow-Wand, had been left also; and the fact that he had a young and delicate girl dependent on him but added to his unhappiness.

Willow-Wand was angry when she was told that they were prisoners, unable to escape from the island, because the boats had been taken away; but she was not afraid, and thought that, if signaled to, the fishermen, who often came to set their nets in the deep and sheltered waters of the bay, would take them off. With the old man's help, she hung a red blanket against the side of the white cliff, in a way that the fishermen would be sure to be attracted when they came again.

Willow-Wand was loved by a young man by the name of Kewe-naw; he had thrown a white doe at the door of her lodge, in token that he desired her for his wife; it had been accepted, and he soon after left the island. Aikie-wai-sie hoped that, when Kewe-naw heard of their desertion, he would come to rescue them; for well the young man knew the dangers to which they were exposed; but Kewe-naw was at the fishing grounds, and might not hear of their plight for months.

This thought caused the old man much anxiety. He was anxious to see his granddaughter wedded to the young man, for he had seen "the glance of love" exchanged between them, and believed that the union would be a happy one.

After satisfying herself that the red signal had been properly placed, by her grandfather's direction Willow-Wand led the way to a hidden ledge in the side of the cliff, where they might watch for the fishermen without being seen themselves. Aikie-wai-sie's fear was that some of the hungry men ot his tribe might return to make a feast off him, and drag Willow-Wand away to a more cruel fate. The ledge they sought was near the cave of the Red Geebis, who fed on nothing but human flesh; and on this account the old man believed they would be secure from any human devils who might look for them. Old and blind as he was, Aikie-wai-sie was ready to fight the whole demon population in defense of his child; but as he feared flesh and blood, he hid from it. A great she-bear slept on the ledge behind them; and Willow-Wand, thinking this a fine opportunity to provide themselves with food, offered to kill it, but the old man forbade.

"There is room for all," he said. "Mockway (bear) offers us no harm. We are not yet in need of food. Let her sleep."

The girl obeyed, and threw herself upon a heap of leaves, which had lately been the bed of the bear, and endeavored to forget her hunger. Their early meal had been but a handful of dried maize and some pounded pemmican; and though the old man had not felt the need of anything more, the girl was suffering for food. The provision in the old man's pouch was scanty, and he hated to draw upon it unnecessarily, so he told her to go to sleep, and, to quiet her, repeated wonderful tales of the Turtle-shaped god, whose robes of state were of brightest green, and whose medicine was always good; of the caves where the souls of giant fairies dwelt until the time when they should be called to perform the last dance; of toadstools which once grew to such great size that the giants used them for lodges; and of how he had once been under the spell of witchcraft himself, and compelled to assume the shape of a reindeer; of how he had shed his horns many times with others of his kind; and how it was only by consenting to entire blindness that he had been permitted to resume his natural shape. He spoke of the beauty of her mother, Whispering Birch; of her wedding with The Willow, a man brave as he was wise, and who early followed his young bride down the misty paths of the dead. Under the soothing influence of his voice the hungry girl fell into a deep sleep.

The sun went down, and though Aikie-waisie's sightless eyes beheld it not, he knew that night was falling by the chilliness of the air. In the darkest night he could tell the direction of the prevailing winds, and the names of the forest trees by passing his hands over their leaves, or by feeling of their bark. Impossible to deceive him. He feared not death, having faced it daily in his life among wild beasts and wilder men; but he feared the evil ones of the cave, not because he was old, but because of his blindness, which prevented his seeing and warning his child when danger assailed them.

There was no moon and no stars in the sky, but a flaming red light from the Devil's Cave streamed over the snowy head of the blind man, and upon the flushed face of the sleeping girl, whose parched lips, even in her dreams, demanded "Water! water!" to relieve her thirst. The anguish of Aikie-wai-sie was almost as great as that of Willow-Wand; for with the "Big Water" lying so near them, it seemed cruel that he could not provide her with drink.

At the girl's feverish mutterings his memory went back to the last hours of her mother, who with her latest breath had confided to him the secret of a magical gift possessed by her child—a gift inherited from her father, The Willow—which, if carefully used, would add great power and many honors to her womanhood. At her command springs of pure water would show themselves, and flow in whatever place or quantity she desired. "This power," said the dying woman, "will bring her great fame as a prophet and healer, but the knowledge of it must not be revealed to her until she becomes a woman."

The old man wondered if this was not the moment to divulge the secret. All things had turned out as Whispering Birch had wished. Her daughter was good and pure and wise beyond her years; she had cared for and provided for all *his* needs, so that the loss of his old wife had not been unendurable. But no; he dared not risk it until she had undergone the fast which should prepare her for a woman's privileges, though he hated to think of the suffering she must endure in the performance of it.

For seven days and nights Willow-Wand endured the pangs of hunger and of thirst; and Aikie-wai-sie, fearing that she would die, and in spite of the danger of being caught by the red devils which infested the place, made his way to the lake to procure the water she so constantly called for. He moistened the poor girl's parched lips and cooled her burning cheeks, but not a drop could he force her to swallow, though "Water! Water!" was ever her delirious cry.

"Nature is working in the child to confirm her mother's words," was the old one's thought; when suddenly in Willow-Wand's breast the "power" rose like a wave, and, leaping to her feet, she struck the outward curving rock, and demanded once more, "Water!"

The old man invoked the aid of the Spirit, and soon heard the musical sound of the tiny stream which ran through the fingers of the surprised girl with a wonderful healing power. Instantly her pains fled, her health returned, and she felt stronger and braver than ever. Remembering her grandfather's need, she quickly gave him of the water, and drank herself until she could drink no more.

When Willow-Wand had broken her fast, she was told the story of her wonderful gift.

A long line of wise women had owned the same power, her grandfather said; but, as she valued her life, she must use it discreetly and reverently and never abuse it. He enumerated the many blessings she would be able to bestow and enjoy; and as he spoke she thought she heard another voice warning her of approaching danger. "Watch!" it said; and as Aikie-wai-sie, worn out with his long vigils, fell into a deep slumber, she concluded to give heed to the warning, and seated herself beside him to "watch" while he slept.

Night came, and she could see the flaming fires of the Devil's Cave, hear the shrieks of the men whom the Geebis were torturing, and the sounds of suffering which she was powerless to alleviate filled her tender heart with pain. The bear crowded nearer to her side, and seemed so sensible of their dangerous situation, and showed such real sorrow for the poor creatures in the cave, that Willow-Wand felt sure that the shaggy-haired animal was one of those unfortunates who had been bewitched by the Evil One, and was glad to have so *human* a thing to keep her company.

The storm increased as the night advanced; black and ragged clouds whirled across the sky; birds of evil omen circled overhead; and creeping things scurried into the crevices of the rocks to escape its fury. "Yen-ad-diz-zee, the crazy gambler, is playing for high stakes to-night," was the girl's thought as she watched the winds striving against each other in the game whose score was marked by lightning strokes or washed away by the rain.

Her heart ached for the unhappy ones who awaited their doom in the fiery pit, and she was wondering if she could not use her magical power in their behalf, when to her horror and dismay she saw Kewe-naw led into the cave and placed near the central fire.

Willow-Wand's shrieks awakened her grandfather, and his grief was great when she told him what had happened. His fears for his own safety and that of his child were increased tenfold, until the bear whispered in his ear, "*Watch*, but fear not."

"The spirit of thy mother lives in this she-bear," he whispered. "Have no fear. Where the spirits of the good abide, no harm can come. Let us obey her commands. *Watch!*"

The girl controlled her grief as well as she could, and threw herself upon the bear's neck to gather comfort from the mother spirit which dwelt within the creature's shaggy breast, while her eyes remained fixed upon the horrors which demons were perpetrating in obedience to the orders of their chief. Young men, whom her people had long given up as dead, were brought in and offered, one after another, in sacrifice to the wicked Manitous, who were ever ready to assist in evil doings, and nightly fed on human flesh as reward for their services.

Terrified lest the next to be cast into the pit should be Kewe-naw, Willow-Wand leapt to her feet with the determination to attempt his rescue. Her movements were noticed by the devils, who recognized her as the "Wand of Power" which their chief desired to possess, and who ordered the infernal ceremonies stopped until he should capture and return with the prize.

In the confusion which followed, it happened that Kewe-naw was left standing near the entrance of the cave, from which place he could see Willow-Wand and her grandfather, in company with the bear, standing on the ledge, while, near by, the chief devil of the pit made his preparations to capture the girl, to whom Kewe-naw was betrothed. Behind him, in the cave, he could distinctly hear the jabberings and demoniac laughter of the loathsome demons, who were finishing up the feast of smoking human flesh which had been interrupted.

The bear, pleased at the unselfishness which had prompted Willow-Wand's act, told Aikie-wai-sie to leave her alone, as all would be well if she were left to follow the promptings of her nature; and when the girl's light and scornful laughter, at the sight of the hideous Geebi endeavoring to make up as a *man* for her conquest, pealed with a thousand musical echoes among the rocks and hills around them, the bear quietly slipped down the steep side of the cliff and disappeared from sight, confident that all would go well with the child and those whom she desired to protect and defend.

The aged man was troubled by the bear's disappearance, but Willow-Wand had no misgivings. "Fear not, my grandfather," she said; "my mother's spirit mingles with my own! Kewe-naw shall be rescued, and to-morrow's sun will look upon our happiness."

The devil had disguised as a warrior whom Aikie-wai-sie and his people feared as one particularly treacherous and bloodthirsty. He thought to terrify the old man into accepting him for his son-in-law, and thought not that Willow-Wand's magical power would be used against him. Well contrived as was his disguise, the girl recognized the devil under it, and scornfully bade him "Begone!" She defied him; and the infuriated monster, forgetting his role, leapt from the projecting rocks to seize the girl, whose power, could he but secure it, would be of inestimable value to him. But Willow-Wand saw him leaping over the crags above her; and as he sprang upon the wall, a single blow of her small hand upon its blistered side brought forth such a gush of water as flung him shrieking into the whirling eddies of the Dead Hole. The fires of the cave were drenched with it, and Kewe-naw began to hope that his life would be saved, even though the Okies and Red Spirits declared that they would rekindle the flames when they had stopped up the holes through which the water poured, and make the roasting pit hotter than ever. Kewe-naw did not believe that they would accomplish this, for he felt that the Spirit of Good was answering his prayers. He looked around for some means of escape; and Willow-Wand, seeing his need, waved a bridge of rainbow mists toward him, by which he safely reached the ledge, to find the girl whom he loved reclining upon the shoulder of her sleeping grandfather, apparently as if nothing unusual had happened.

The eastern sky showed streaks of red as Kewe-naw seated himself beside the old man to await his awakening. With a knife taken from her grandfather's belt, Willow-Wand cut the thongs which bound his arms, prepared a pipe for his smoking, and left him.

No word of welcome or joyful greeting was uttered by these grave lovers; no trembling of *his* hand, no glance of *her* eye, spoke the happiness they felt.

All day the grandfather slept, all day the lover smoked, and all day the maiden *worked* to clear the cave of its remaining horrors. She flung the howling demons into the lake, and quenched the smouldering fires of the pit, that they might do no further harm; and it was late when she returned to the ledge to share her lover's vigil.

Evening came. Aikie-wai-sie woke to find the desire of his heart fulfilled. The lovers embraced; he gave them his blessing, and joined their hands in marriage.

Kewe-naw told the story of his adventures. He had been under an evil spell. The fishing season being over, he set sail for the island to join his people before they left for the winter; his boat, capsized by a sudden squall, went to the bottom as if made of iron, and he was thinking that he must soon have to follow it, because impossible to swim long in such a storm, when he saw a pair of moccasins floating before him on the crests of the waves. He put his feet into them, only to find them shod with lightning, which bore him in a flash to the cave from which he had just escaped.

Willow-Wand then related to him something of the gift of which she had become possessed; and of how she had driven the devils from the cave and made the bridge by which he had escaped. Then she told him of the day spent in making the cave habitable, and that with his help she hoped to make a comfortable home there.

The red blanket had not brought the fishermen as soon as expected, but when they did come Ke-we-naw purchased one of their boats, and with their assistance soon conveyed to his cave the store of provisions which he had prepared for winter use. Pemmican, dried venison and bears' meat, and fruits which he had found time to collect and dry between the "setting" and "taking" of the nets, were among the good things of their larder; and with rush mats for the floors, sacks of leaves and pine needles for couches, and warm furs for clothing and coverings, they looked forward to the winter without fear.

The Devil's fuel, *for once*, was put to good use, enough being found in the recesses of the cave to last them a lifetime; with it the new home was made warm and comfortable; and here the young couple passed the first happy months of their married life.

The Indians returned in the spring to find Aikie-wai-sie living contentedly amid the comforts which his children provided; and when they were told that Willow-Wand had worked all the changes by a powerful magic which she possessed, they easily believed it, and said that "nothing but magic could banish evil spirits and make a happy home out of what was once a place of torment;" but when the young couple showed them the whirling pool which lay between the "Island of the Round Game" and their own, and they saw the bodies of the demons rise to the surface of the water in proof of what Willow-Wand's power had done, they were at once accepted as prophets whose "medicine was good."

The Cave of the Red Geebis is marked in the guide books as Devil's Kitchen, from the fact that Indians were known to have roasted and feasted upon human flesh there.

SUGAR LOAF.

NATURE is too lovely at Mackinac to permit the mind doing other service than to admire; and so, sheltered from the summer winds which tan our cheeks, freckle our noses, and ruffle our hair, we stretch full length upon the mosses of the deep ravine which gives soft welcome to our weary limbs, while we listen to the "tales of woe" which we have journeyed to this enchanted ground to hear from the lips of a real live Indian.

The Sugar Loaf stands guard in a thickly-wooded plateau, the admiration and veneration of ages; and with eyes fixed upon its summit, where clings a giant cedar—hanging by old gnarled roots upon its crumbling holding, as if for dear life—we hearken to the wondrous histories which stumble from the lips of the aged man, who is a character of some renown in this region, and often employed as interpreter by the natives. He is grave and reserved and *cross-eyed*, and to him, like his eyes, the world seems sadly mixed. It is perhaps not strange that his stories, ancient or modern, should correspond with his feelings.

The Sugar Loaf, he says, was so called from the fact that the bees once made a gigantic hive of the rock. The cave, which extends through it from base to summit, and every crack, pocket, or ledge, was filled with honey of the purest kind, supplying the Indians most generously with this delicious article of food.

This story was common in the old man's

time, and often had he probed the cells and crevices of the soft rock for sweets, which he declared both he and his mother and his grandmother before him had always found there in plenty, and which his people had believed would never be exhausted.

Another story is that the conical rocks of the Island are the transformed bodies of the Giants who once dwelt there. The Indians believe that the Giants will return to life when Hiawatha comes again. The squaws place propitiatory offerings upon the rocks, and always resort to them for help in times of sickness.

THE MANITOUS.

[NOTE.—Miss Martha Tanner was authority for this legend, which she chanted for my pen. The legend explains the reverence in which the rocks were held, two of which resembled the human form, the other a dog.]

ONE was a boy and one was a girl, and one was a dog; the boy and the girl were lovers, and the dog loved both. The Indian loves his home; the Indian loves the lodge of his wife and babes; the Indian loves the moss-covered graves of his fathers, mouldered and gone; but the boy and the girl loved more. The warrior loves the shout of his foe; the warrior loves the festival of scalps; the hunter to see the wings of the plover beating the air; but the lovers loved more.

They were betrothed in their cradles, and grew up as lovers. The maiden grew to be tall as the chin of a lofty man, beautiful and bright as the star which shines to guide the hunter through the wilds to his home; but the boy got no strength with the years—took no pleasure in the chase—painted not as the warriors paint, red on the cheek and brow—and he was deemed an unfit husband for the girl. She was told by her father that the pledge must be broken.

My brother hears?

What said the youth when he heard the stern command which broke his being's strongest bond as ye break an untwisted rope of grass?

The waters of sorrow gushed out at his eyes, and waves of grief drowned his soul! When the evening mists walked out of the earth, he left his lodge with an aching heart, and wandered forth with his dog. To the lonely, dim, and silent woods he went to weep and pray; the heaven of his life was dark, and he wept with fear. Like a dumb creature of the forest he mourned the loss of his mate; to his bones was he smitten and hurt with his loss, and weak as a blasted thing of dust; into the silent woods he fled, to hide like a bird from the storm.

Weary, he sleeps and dreams. Down the misty, sleep-wrapped paths of the Silent Land he sweeps to kneel before the spirit of his guardian shape, whose care he is, who loves him as a mother loves the babe at her breast, as the father loves the child of his age, who hopes for him as love hopes, and waits, but dies not. He dreams, and the maiden floats to his side in a veil of stars.

He woke. Whom saw he near?

My brother hears?

He saw the maiden so well beloved, with hair like the grape-clustered vine, whose throat was that of the swan, whose eyes were mild as the dove's, whose hand was the span of the red oak's leaf, whose foot was the length of the lark's spread wing, whose step was as swift as the wild gazelle's, whose voice was the voice of singing rill—but, oh, how changed! Beaming eye and bounding foot the maiden hath no more. Slow is her step as a crippled bird's, and mournful her voice as the dying sigh of the breeze; and yet she joys to see the youth. He calls her name, and into his arms she flies like a fawn which escapes the hunter's shaft and reaches its dam unhurt. Evening veils their meeting lips, as, locked in a soft and warm embrace, the lovers recline on a mossy bank and pledge their vows anew. Loudly they call on the host of stars, and the cold and dimly shining moon, and the spirits that watch by night in the air, or chirp in the hollow rock, to see the plighting of their hands.

My brother hears?

They married *themselves*, and man and wife became in the wilderness. Never shall they return to the lodge of their fathers, and never shall they grow old, worshiped by my people as the symbol of youth and love and faithfulness. Thus it was that they became gods.

DEVIL'S LAKE.

AT the west end of Mackinac Island there was once a small but very deep piece of water, known by the Indians to have been the home of an evil Manitou. This pond or bog is now dry, but the hollow where it once lay is still called Devil's Lake, and being situated just above the Devil's Kitchen, the latter place no doubt derived its name from the old lake, the source of the inexhaustible supply of water which still drips clear as crystal from its hidden springs, or runs in musical little rills from innumerable natural mains among the "top shelves and wall pockets," the indispensable adjuncts of even a *Devil's* Kitchen.

Devil's Lake was regarded with awe by the dusky inhabitants, as it was believed to be bottomless; the body of any one drowned there never having been recovered. Superstition still lives among the Indians and their descendants there, and will die hard; especially that those superstitions regarding the power of their Medicine Men and Wise Women, and the spells cast for them by the many Manitous, good or evil, are still in existence, is without doubt.

There are many traditions concerning Devil's Lake, some true, others fabulous, and also many songs of love, revenge, or hate associated with it; and it is with great satisfaction that these people find that Devil's Lake is entirely dry, a lake no more. It was a custom of the Indians to kill their crippled children, as they believed that a distorted body was an impersonation of God's anger, a creature set apart for scorn and loathing, and many a poor little "hunchback" for this reason has lost its life in the deep water of Devil's Lake. This "deep water" is said to have been the abode of an evil god, who attracted persons to its edge by sweet singing, and then bore them to his submarine home, there to remain forever.

The tradition is that the young and lovely wife of Little Rail came one evening to bathe in the "musical water;" but as she was a stranger to the place and to her husband's people, she was ignorant of the "bad medicine" in it. The evening was warm and still, and the overhanging gray clouds which drifted and swayed to the rhythmic measures which floated over the water foretold a storm. Being a good swimmer the young woman was entirely without fear, and after removing a wonderful garment of feathers which she wore, stepped as lightly and calmly into the darkening pool as if the sun was shining brightly. The soft mosses welcomed her tiny feet, the odorous branches of the trees which grew upon the shore reached down to fan the spicy air about her, and the breeze which ruffled its edges played about her lithe limbs as if pleased to bear so fair a thing upon its bosom. So sweet was she that all the sweetest airs of heaven wandered happily confused, or loitered blissfully among her abundant beauties.

The swallows who had ceased their happy nest-building to watch the beauteous human creature at her bath, took fright at the ragged clouds which scudded across the sky, and dipping and darting, circling and wheeling in the thickening air, sought the dense foliage of the trees for safety; and it was only when the flying clouds burst in wild gusts upon her, and she saw the untamed creatures of the forest lose heart and crouch trembling beneath the rocks which edged the shore, as if they feared the lashing of the branches of their forest home and would escape a whipping by taking shelter there, that she felt herself to be in danger.

Thunder rolled along the heavens and lightnings flashed from among the whirling clouds as she hurried from the water, and hastily replaced her dress of feathers, in the hope that she might reach her lodge before the rain should fall.

She was just about leaving the place when a flash of lightning revealed to her terrified gaze a fearful shape moving toward her from the lake, which no longer gave forth delicious music, but howled and raged in the gathering gloom, its deep bosom shaking, its writhing wavelips sending most awful and gruesome shrieks after the monster Geebis, who was about to land upon the beach at her feet. She turned to fly from the place, but she could move neither hand nor foot—she was fixed to the spot.

The creature was more beast than man, having the face and head of a human being, ornamented by a pair of cow's horns; the body was that of an ox, upon which grew long stiff hair, like that of a goat; the hoofs were cloven, but the limbs and hands were those of a man. A peculiar bluish and altogether wonderful light enveloped the shape, and shed its luminance for yards around. The hideous devil caught the young wife in his powerful arms, and while uttering awful peals of demoniac laughter, stripped her of her beautiful plumage, and cried out with fiendish joy at the spoiling of each feather.

"Ah! ha! I see through thy strange garment! I read thy feathers! I see through them, to the golden heart in thy breast. Thou must henceforth serve *me!*"

Smitten to the heart with fear, and, though unable to move, having all her senses and perfectly understanding that she was under an evil spell, she gave herself heart and mind to the Master of Life, hoping that if *her* life were this night to be required of her, the sacrifice might benefit some dear ones in the earthly garden from whence she was to be taken. Her misery was increased when she saw her husband approaching, now clearly, now darkly, as the wonderful light which emanated from the monster alternately flashed and faded upon his path, as she was unable to warn him of his danger.

When Little Rail caught sight of his beloved bride in the clutches of the horrible beast, he flew to her rescue, leaped upon the monster, and with a cry of rage for every blow which his strong arm rained sharply and swiftly upon the Geebis, he gave battle; but his efforts were unavailing. The fight was against unseen powers, and useless against such odds. With a gesture of despair at his failure to make the creature let go his hold, Little Rail urged his wife to *free herself* from the embrace of the Devil, and fly to the sacred land upon which the Evil One dared not set foot; but the unhappy woman could only tell of her miserable enchantment by the language of her tender and compassionate eyes, which her husband had not until then understood.

The Devil shrieked with rage at the attempted rescue, threatening the life of his victim as he waved the plumed gown several times above her head, thus completing her subjugation, and commanded that she should dance for him the various dances of her people; after which he announced that it was his intention to take her to his home at the bottom of the lake.

Her limbs relaxed and became supple enough to admit of her performing some steps before the dreadful Manitou. Her will being entirely under his control, she could not refuse to do his bidding; but in obeying she broke an unwritten law of her people, as dances were performed only at set seasons and for the celebration of feasts, and were not of ordinary nor frequent occurrence. The Devil was not pleased with her efforts, and she at last concluded to shorten the misery of her husband by dancing the Death Dance, though by doing so she felt that she sealed her own doom. When she glided into its measured paces, the Devil muttered his gratification; but Little Rail watched the proceeding with an aching heart and streaming eyes. He pleaded in vain for the life of his bride; the Devil would not listen, and cruelly informed the sorrowing husband that he was about to see his wife descend to the bottom of the lake, and added to his cruelty by saying that when the lake was dry land, but not before, he should be reunited to her. The Devil then cast the helpless woman into the "deep water," and remained for hours near the place hurling stones upon her, lest she should rise once more. When he was about to disappear beneath the waves himself, he turned upon the grief-stricken Little Rail, who sat on the rocks with his head between his knees to hide his tearful eyes, and with a twist of his strong, bony fingers, broke the poor fellow's back, so that Little Rail was a "hunch-back" from that day.

The pain and grief of Little Rail was great, but he bore it with fortitude, and vowed to be true to his lost bride; and, to hasten the day of their reunion, at once began to throw stones into the pond, with the purpose of filling it up. He believed, if this were accomplished, that his wife would be restored to him; for a Manitou, good or bad, never breaks his word. Little Rail enlisted in the service all kind-hearted and sympathetic ones, and especially did he plead for the assistance of the children; and it soon became the custom—an act of devotion, prayer, or penance—to cast into the lake a certain number of pebbles for small offenses, stones and great boulders for greater sins, and an additional stone each time for the joining of the two faithful souls. After a time whole tribes of Indians would journey to the lake to perform their stone-throwing penances, and when the time came for dropping one for the long-separated couple, there was much laughter and merry-making among them.

On still nights it is said that the voice of the Evil Manitou could be heard laughing derisively at the indefatigable toil of the husband, and often caused so much annoyance that it was necessary to have some worthy Medicine Man quell the boisterous spirit by incantations.

It is a long time now since the voice of the Evil Manitou has been heard. His so-called fathomless home is at last filled up—lost to sight forever—and thus the reunion of the Little Rail and his bride is assured, if Manitous keep their promises and tradition speaks true. But Little Rail will never regain his comely figure, but will always remain a *broken-backed* little duck.

FORT HOLMES.

LIFTED on this stately rising is an observatory, constructed and kept in repair by Governmental powers. At the foot of this structure, in the hollow of an old magazine, one can rest secure from rough winds; or, reclining upon its outer rim, breathe in an air as light as nitrous gas, where naught is seen but billowy waves of green, which encircle it on every side, and may perhaps be moved to invoke the Indian muse.

From this hill-top—Fort Holmes—named for the gallant officer who was "here laid low," the faithful Mecostewanda daily watched and waited for the return of her husband, who had gone upon the war-path. Che-to-wait was a warrior as wise as he was brave; and because his ghost did not appear to her, Mecostewanda could not believe that he was dead. She sent her four sons, each in a different direction, to bring her news of him, but they returned unsuccessful.

One evening, while the early moon was still pale, and the western sky was blushing from the farewell kisses of the sun, Mecostewanda saw a strange craft going slowly by the rock on which she sat. The sides of the boat were of stone, its sails were feathered wings, and its shape that of a canoe; at the oars toiled a stalwart brave, stripped and painted for war; while at the bow, enveloped in a gray blanket, stood an aged man, who pointed with the long rod which he held the course they were to take.

The voice of the rower floated to her, bearing the words of the Death Song. The voice and the song were Che-to-wait's, and by it the faithful woman was at last convinced that her children were fatherless and herself a widow.

HIAWATHA.

THE Island of Mackinac—that gem of beauty which binds the lakes—is believed by the Indians to be the first batch of earth the Great Spirit ever made. Others have it that when the first earth had been heaped by the winds upon the back of the Great Turtle, which had its home at that particular spot in the primeval ocean, and had become the first island or the beginning of the world, that God Himself was born there, and that there the Giants dwelt, whose parents, the Indian Adam and Eve, came from the "Heart of the Sun."

Hiawatha, the Indian Messiah, was born there, and had his home in the caverns which the waves had worn in the limestone cliffs of the Eastern shore, where the winds whispered in his "clear ear" things undreamed of by the Red Men before. They told him the story of his father's marriage with Wenona, the Child of the Star—of how he had won her love, and after she had given him four sons, treated her with such cruelty that she died.

Hiawatha followed his father to the edge of the world, and fought a long and terrible battle with him to avenge his mother's wrongs; but his father, being invincible, could not be vanquished, and a reconciliation took place between them.

The father, to prove the sincerity of his feelings, endowed Hiawatha with his own everlasting strength and invincible powers,

HIAWATHA

and sent him back to the Island of the Straits to teach his people the wonderful things he had learned.

On his return journey, Hiawatha lodged for a few days with an Arrow-maker of the Dacotahs, whose soft-voiced daughter, Minniehaha (Laughing Water), assisted him in the manufacture of his wares.

At any time, and in any place, Love's wings may flutter; and now for the first time in the soul of Hiawatha Love sang its Meaning Song. He declared his love, the Arrow-maker's daughter returned it, and they continued the journey to the island as man and wife.

He called a council of his friends and brothers, and taught them all good laws. He formed them into clans and nations, and sent them forth to people the earth. In the primitive Indians, courage and fortitude, perseverance and justice and brotherly love, were inbred; but the teachings of Hiawatha added a knowledge of the arts and sciences and all crafts. Fasting and praying he made obligatory, as such acts of faith opened the mind for the reception of the knowledge which Hiawatha spent his life in expounding.

By a word Hiawatha could change himself into whatever creature he wished. His powers were as wonderful as they were varied. He cut off the scalp-lock of an enemy and planted it for tobacco. His wife, by drawing off her garments, and under cover of darkness running naked with them in her hand three times around the cornfields, made them fertile.

Minniehaha was a beautiful woman, and a loving and faithful wife to her gifted husband. She died of the plague; and Hiawatha, who could not keep his heart from following the woman who had made him happy, soon followed her. With his last breath he commanded his people to live uprightly, to avoid bloodshed, and to live in peace and love.

As he was lifted into the sky, the promise to return to them fell from his lips. Those lips had never told them a lie, and the belief of the Indians in the coming of this Messiah is as strong to-day as when the promise was made.

When the Northern Lights are seen, streaking the heavens with their rose and yellow, the Indians of Lake Superior, where Hiawatha was buried, say that "He is gathering his army from among the warriors of the upper world;" and they hold themselves in readiness for the word of command to join the spirits in their march upon their natural enemies, the pale-faces, to assist in their extermination. Upon the return of Hiawatha the entire white population is to be destroyed, and the Indians are once more to occupy the land of their fathers, in affluence and power.

THE CRACK.

STORY OF THE GIANT'S FINGERS.

MACKINAC ISLAND was once the home of a band of red-skinned giants, of whom Hiawatha was the chief. When these giants passed from the earth, they became "waiting spirits," or "wandering demons," according to the judgment of the Master of Souls: if the former, they took the shape of conical rocks, pinnacles, or boulders; and if the latter, they were given the forms of men of the most heartless and unfeeling disposition and nature. Many stories are told concerning them.

Near "Wacheo"—a part of Hubbard's Annex—is a field of several acres belonging to the Government; and splitting its level ground from end to end is a deep and mysterious chasm, put down in the guide books as the "Crack." A frightful place, full of dark shadows and mournful echoings, which no man ever penetrated successfully, its steep sides offering no foothold; and of the unwary ones who have stumbled headlong into the "Crack," none have returned to tell its mysteries.

Indians, or half-breed hunters or trappers, are superstitious in regard to taking game from this locality; they avoid the place, and would refuse to eat of food procured there, if starving. Sight-seeing tourists who have the curiosity to examine the place, do so at the

the discomfort of life-lines and other paraphernalia of safety.

The tradition is that this crack is haunted by a giant demon, who was so foolish as to wish to penetrate the Under Land where the Spirits of the Dead held sway. This of course was not permitted, and the Giant's Fingers were never released from the fissure in the rock where he clung, and from which those who have *good eyes* declare he may still be seen hanging above the abyss.

Five immense fingers, the knuckles, back of the hand, and wrist are still distinctly visible beneath the scales of limestone with which the ages have covered them. It is believed that the curse of the Giant falls upon those who by accident or design tread upon his clinging digits. Sickness, blindness, loss of wealth, misfortune in love affairs being among the dire calamities brought by contact with the demon, who, though a prisoner undergoing punishment, has still a malignant power which he does not hesitate to use.

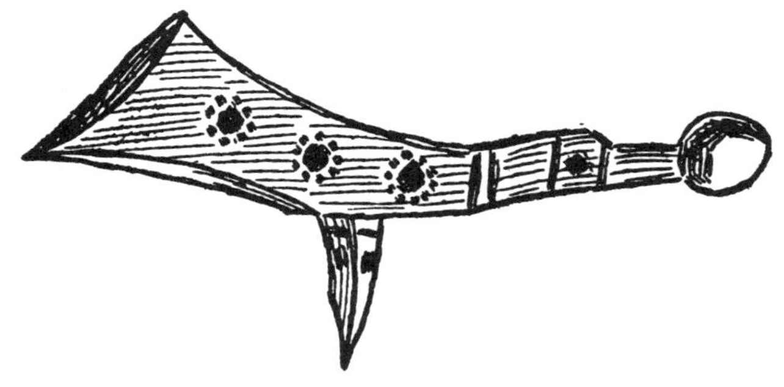

VENGEANCE OF SPY BUCK.

A STORY is told of hate and revenge, coupled with enduring love and faithfulness on the part of two braves, who in youth were friends closer than brothers. One could see no fault in the other, and until both loved the same woman, naught of distrust or untruth marred their friendship.

Black Bear was of a calm and contemplative nature, strong in his affections; no man ever attributed to him any meanness, and his bravery was unquestioned. Spy Buck, on the other hand, was of a fiery disposition, quick to resent even the suspicion of insult; on the word, without rhyme or reason, he was ready for war. These two men were friends, and they loved the same woman.

The maiden was beautiful, but unworthy of either of her lovers; both wore amulets of her making, and she played fast and loose with them for a long time, until one evening Black Bear came upon his friend where he sat in the twilight, playing upon the flute to attract the attention and love of the maiden whom he believed to be faithfully pledged to himself; and not until he saw the beloved of his heart come shyly forth from her wigwam and nestle softly to the side of him whom he called by the name of a friend, could he believe in her perfidy.

He sickened at the thought of wearing so polluted a flower, a flower whose fragrance had been *sniffed*, and whose velvety softness had been ruffled by another lover. His faithful heart would forever treasure the *memory* of his love; but the woman for whom he bore it had lain in the arms of another lover, and to that other she must henceforth cleave. He no longer claimed her; she belonged to his friend.

The cry of shame and fear which fell from the lips of the guilty girl, as her eyes encountered those of Black Bear, as he neared them in the deepening shadows of the wood, was all that was required to inform Spy Buck as to how matters stood between the trembling maiden whom he still clasped in his arms, and Black Bear. In an instant he hated him with an unquenchable hate; and that Black Bear uttered no word of sorrow or complaint to the dear ones, who had until now been his life's anchors, only infuriated Spy Buck more. With clenched hands and veins swollen with rage, he dashed down the narrow path to fall upon and tear him to pieces; but Black Bear stepped gravely out of the way, saying simply:

"I loved you and I leave you."

Black Bear's intention was to leave the island and make his home with those of his nation who dwelt on the mainland; but before his arrangements were completed he was arrested and taken before his chief to answer to the charge of conspiracy to betray the Indians to the English with whom the tribes were at war.

At the intercession of his false love his life was spared, and at night when the old men were sitting in council to determine upon Black Bear's sentence, the unhappy girl came to his place of imprisonment to implore his forgiveness. In frightened whispers she confessed that appearances were against her, but that she loved him alone and would never wed any other. She told him how Spy Buck, through jealousy and a desire for revenge, had made the charges against him, which but for her would have cost him his life. She wept at the thought of what her folly had brought about, and begged Black Bear to believe her words. But he would not listen to her "tales of deceit;" he still trusted Spy Buck, but he could not renew his confidence in the girl who had fooled him. Nevertheless he sorrowed for her and forgave her.

His life was spared; but to prevent his ever taking arms again, it was ordered that his right hand be severed at the wrist. To this ruling Black Bear yielded without hesitation, and went through the ordeal without a tremor; but when it was declared by the head chief in his hearing that his good right hand was to be given as a trophy of honor to Spy Buck, his faith in his friend was staggered.

Were the words of his false love true? Had Spy Buck done this thing? He wished not to believe it, and called upon his friend to refute the story, but he was commanded to be silent. He was in disgrace, and no one listened to him.

In a fury of jealous hate at the sight of the girl whom he loved, in company with the condemned—for she alone of all the people remained near him—Spy Buck took the "trophy of honor" and strutted about among the crowd to exhibit it. A laugh was raised at the expense of the unhappy pair standing apart from the rest, and to add to the amusement Spy Buck struck them both in the face with the clay-cold hand in which he so often had laid his own with promises of truth. Black Bear resented not the insult, though the people fully expected to witness an encounter between the two, and were surprised to see him wave his maimed arm as his excuse for not gratifying them in that respect; and then, before them all, with all the courage of unmerited dishonor, take the maiden by the hand and lead her to the door of Spy Buck's lodge, saying as he left her: "This is your place—here you must suffer." He embarked that same day in a canoe and sailed away, never to return. But through all the long years of his exile his relentless foe followed him with increased hate and acts of cruel vengeance, and not until he had lived to be a poor and feeble old man, cut off from faith and love, and all that makes life worth living, did he learn that Spy Buck had not won the maiden who had caused his downfall.

One evening, when the first snow sprinkled the ground, and hungry crows cawed dismally from among the frozen branches, or flapped their wings against the shabby lodge, over whose small fire Black Bear hung in the vain effort to warm his benumbed limbs, a feeble and wrinkled old woman lifted the curtain, and in stooping to enter, fell swooning at his feet. His eyes, dim with grief and famine, recognized at once the love of his youth. She had come to die with him. He clasped her to his aching heart—again and again he pressed her to him with all the ardor of his youthful passion. He called her name! He looked into her eyes. They were glazed with death. He needed not the Medicine Man to tell him this. Once more he pressed her to his heart, and then, his feeble hold relaxing, they fell together to the ground. Dimly, through the mists which veiled his dying eyes, he saw the tall form of Spy Buck bending above them, and with a last effort to shield the woman from the knife which flashed in his uplifted hand, bent his withered frame above her body, and so died. Morning found the aged pair smiling peacefully in the sleep of death; the poisoned blade, which had not hastened death a moment, bound their bodies heart to heart. At the door lay all that remained of Spy Buck, with the dogs snarling over the bits of flesh still left upon his bones.

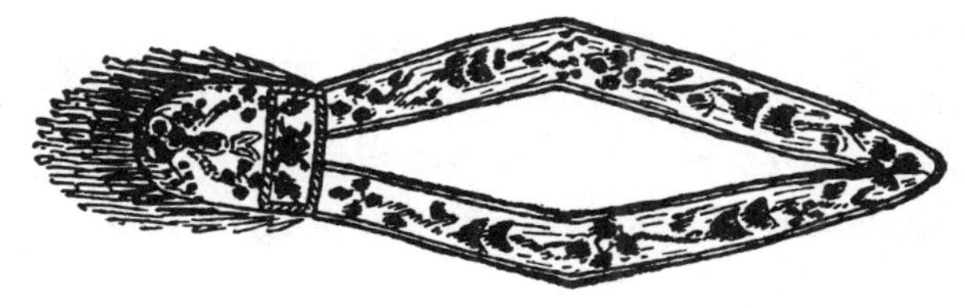

LEGEND OF THE CLEAR WATER.

(Wishing Well.)

IN the days of this story, there lived at Manitoulin a wise and influential chief by the name of Menehwehna, the father of a beautiful daughter, who was a constant source of delight and anxiety to him. The mother was dead. The daughter was named Ish-ko-dah, the fiery. The women of her tribe all looked upon her with envy on account of her great beauty, and also because she was a favorite with the young men, and had already been sought in marriage by the most eligible of them.

To Menehwehna's regret, the fiery-tempered girl had turned from her wooers in contempt. The old man felt that his years could not now be many more upon the earth, and he desired to see his child housed in a lodge of her own, with a husband to provide for her needs, before he should pass to the Place of Souls. He cared not that Ishkodah should be friendly with the women, but he was greatly grieved that the ear of his child was deaf to tales of love. To him it seemed that her heart was as cold as the stones on the shore, her eyes as soulless as the eyes of the dead.

"Love can not touch her," the old man thought; and, determining to take matters into his own hands, commanded Ishkodah to accept her next offer, and set about making a choice for her without delay.

The young brave whom he selected as a husband for Ishkodah was of great skill and courage, and came of a long ancestral line. His name was Wa-bas-so—"Nimble Foot." Menehwehna invited him to pay them a visit, promising a royal welcome, and told his daughter to prepare for her betrothal. Ish-ko-dah, who loved as well as feared her old father, obeyed at once, though surprised at his interference in her affairs.

On his arrival at their village Ishkodah caught a passing glimpse of the young man whom she had been ordered to wed, but that was enough. She had seen her master, and loved him at once. When the girl came and stood before Menehwehna in all the gay apparel which she had made for her betrothal, he started in wonder at her beauty and grace, to which was added a charm delightful to behold; a spirit shone in her eyes hitherto unseen, a lightness of step as she moved over the mossy turf, a tone in the voice sweeter than ever. He was not long in learning the cause of the change. Ishkodah loved.

The old father took her trembling hand in his, and to his joy the clasp was lovingly returned. Love sent the blood, which had run so sluggishly before, bounding through the veins.

"Daughter," he said, "I no longer mourn thee as without heart. A lover hath once more lifted his eyes to thee. What hast thou to say to him?"

"My father, I already love the youth."

"Hast thou seen the young chieftain who would lift the curtain of thy lodge?"

"I have seen him, and the spirit which holds the way to my heart hath given him to possess it, and all that I am."

"The spirits of the upper air have ever been his guide—" but she interrupted her father, knowing his thought.

"Enough. It is the same with me in any case. I love him, and him would I have wedded if his face were painted in colors of woe, if his spear were never raised from the ground. I have seen him, and I shall build his fire, sweep his lodge, and prepare his food, though the Bird of Thunder and War hover ever over our bed!"

This outburst was gravely checked by the old chief, who advised Ishkodah to beware of uttering such sentiments in the hearing of Wabasso.

"The young brave who will seek thee when the daylight hath faded from the earth hath ever lived under the guidance of that Great Spirit called the Good, and it will be well for thee to remain in silent subjection to thy husband."

Evening slipped over the edge of night, and the youth stood at the door of Ishkodah's lodge. Downcast eyes and smiling lips were his welcome. He glided into the vacant seat at her side, and threw about her the Blanket of Love in which he was enveloped. She sank within his warm embrace as gladly and trustfully as the young fawn reclines beside its dam. Joy filled their hearts, and peace reigned in their lodge.

The story of their wedded happiness went throughout the whole nation. Ishkodah followed her old father's advice, and remained in silent subjection to her husband, who named her Main-wain-dum-e-yum—*Thou makest me happy*. Particularly did the young wife give heed to her father's injunctions as regarded her religious faith, and on this subject was also silent. She *felt* to thank the Spirit of Good who had influenced her to love the young warrior, whom she believed to be a gift direct from Michabou; but her pride forbade, so she returned no thanks for the gift, and looked not above the earth for happiness. Her father finding that she was obedient to his commands, gave her a name signifying "She of the Silent Tongue," and all went well while the old man lived; but one day Ishkodah was called upon to say a last farewell to the friend who, of all others save her warrior husband, was most interested in her welfare; and she stood by the side of her dying father to receive his last words—*commands* which she must obey or die.

"Let thy tongue continue its silence that thy beauty may last forever," said the dying chief. "If neither doubt nor distrust enter thy heart, thou and thy husband shall live till thy feet are worn out with walking, thy mouths with eating; and when Pauguk comes for thee thou shalt cross the Black Water in a stone canoe like that of thy husband, that thou mayst be near him in the flood which surrounds the place to which thou journeyest. Together thou shalt reach tbe Happy Island, if thou my daughter hast obeyed my words. Call upon the Good when thou art in need. Neglect to do so, and thou shalt never reach thy journey's end, but sink to thy chin in the Black Water, to spend the hours of eternity witnessing the bliss of thy husband, when he hath received the reward which awaits all those who have paid the tribute of praise to the 'Master of Life.'"

And so he died.

When they had buried him, Main-wain-dum-e-yum returned to her home, saying softly to herself: "I have nothing to fear; I shall obey my father's words. I need not fear death, for I shall not walk far nor eat that which shall be hurtful. Silence is all that is required of me. I shall live forever."

Soon after this a great trouble came to her. She was to be parted from her husband whom she must love and never doubt.

Wabasso was known to be the bravest man of his tribe, yet his courage failed and sorrow looked out of his eyes as they dwelt upon the young wife whom he was now to leave for the first time since he had given her the pledge of love. With a heavy heart he announced his departure.

"When morning comes up from among the red clouds of the east, I must join the young men who go forth upon the warpath. I am a great brave, and must be among the foremost of them; and yet I grieve to leave thee. Keep thou thy lodge until my return, when thou shalt wear the trophies of victory I bring to thee. Thou shalt deck thyself once more in thy wedding garments, and for my pleasure shalt sing thy thanks to the Great Spirit who gives us to triumph over our enemies."

She-of-the-Silent-Tongue mourned for his going, and desired to know the term of his absence.

"Two moons shall shine and wane upon the earth ere I return. I have given to thee the pledge of faithfulness, and I here renew it by the eternal stars which light the heavens; but no pledge do I require of thee, thy lodge shall keep thee safe till my coming. Thou lovest me well. Keep thy tongue silent, and I shall return to find a fire of welcome on thy hearth, where I may warm, whilst thou shalt revive me with thy loving arms."

He departed.

One moon had slowly waned, and Main-wain-dum-e-yum pined so for her lover that at last the silence of the home lodge became intolerable to her, and she began to visit the women whose husbands and sons had followed Wabasso to the wars; but their loneliness made her heart even heavier than before, and she soon left them to themselves. Forgetting the counsel of her father, she set out for the cave of an old woman, who could foretell events, to learn something of Wabasso's fortunes—if he were well, and whether he would be successful in his undertakings, but, above all, the day of his return.

Guh was especially wicked and malevolent in her dealings with Ishkodah. She had an old grudge against Menehwehna, and by bringing about the downfall of his proud daughter she intended to revenge herself. Guh knew well why silence had been enjoined upon Ishkodah, and determined to make her knowledge serve the purpose of her revenge.

"Guh," (mother) said the lonely girl, "I am sick with longing! Another moon must drag its shining trail around the earth ere our young men return! My soul is in darkness, my dreams clouded; give me of thy mystic potion that I may sleep until my husband comes again. Give me good dreams that I may not die!"

"Ugh!" ejaculated the wise woman; "thou mayst drink if thou wilt, but I can not be responsible for thy dreams! Impossible is it for me to govern the wild thoughts of the proud Ishkodah; but be thy dreams good or evil, they will be true."

Now Guh had two secret potions—one for producing good, and the other for producing bad dreams. She gave of the latter to Ishkodah, who drank of it, while she mumbled tales of the beautiful pale-faced women who captured the hearts of Indians, and lured them away from home and honor.

She who had made happy the heart of Wabasso heard as one stunned, or as one half sleeping, the whispered insinuations of Guh. A sort of lethargy crept over her mind, from which she partly roused, and drowsily bent her steps homeward, there to sleep deeply, and if possible forget the jealous thoughts which had been implanted in her heart.

Every squaw in the village was soon aware that the silence which Ishkodah, the once fiery-tempered girl, had preserved toward them for so long had been broken, and were all chattering over it, and laughing to think how the mate of their chief had fallen from her high place among them and come under the spell of the Witch Woman.

Main-wain-dum-e-yum had indeed drunk deeply of the potion which Guh concocted for her. She slept. She dreamed; and when the effect of the drug wore off, she drank again and again, and for many nights and days she existed without further nourishment. In dreams she saw her husband hurrying toward her with something in his hand, upon which he gazed as he advanced. Drawing near, she saw the ear of *red corn*, perfect in shape and brilliant in color, which held his fascinated gaze. This proved to the unhappy dreamer that some woman admired her husband, or else, alas! that he had given his love to another, and would never return to her. The thought that it might be herself to whom the corn pointed, or that Wabasso was seeking by the aid of the magical ear of corn to know of the welfare of his wife, came not to brighten the darkness of her thought. Guh's baneful drink governed her dreams; truths were lies, good was bad; in short, the whole nature of the girl was perverted. The sight of the ear of red corn, believing as she did in its evil tendency, sickened Ishkodah to nausea and produced intense pains in her head. Once more she gave herself of the potion to ease her agony, and again she saw her lover and dreamed the same dream. A voice said, "Go to the *Clear Water*. See for thyself. Be convinced."

Obedient, she left her bed and staggered along the rough beach to find the path which led to the Clear Water, and which her dream told her lay beneath a dizzy cliff.

The musical rustling of the leaves of the trees soothed the tired brain of the dreamer; the joyous singing of the birds and their bright plumage diverted her thoughts, and there came a moment when the music of their voices and their playful innocent twitterings as they flew about her pressed upon her the remembrance of her evil course, her disobedience and disloyalty. She was on the point of turning back. The stillness of the woods, the odor of the spicy trees, the fragrant-smelling flowers, all combined to quiet her, to influence her to give up the unlawful thing which she was about to do, to return to her neglected lodge and there wait in patience for her husband's coming. For a moment she was moved to do so, but the thought of the pale woman who might at this moment be winning her lover from her returned, and sent her madly on her way once more. The good spirits did not desert her without another effort; they reminded her of her father's words, of Wabasso's faithfulness and trust in her. "But, oh!" she answered, "to see for myself those loved and living eyes look back at me from the clear depths of fortune's pool!" and she sprang lightly onward, the sooner to receive the confirming testimony.

Dark spirits hovered near as she gained the deeper woods, though no fear of Geebis, hobgoblin, or blue spirit had as yet troubled her dream. She had never known fear; her only religion had been her love for Wabasso, whom she made happy. Why fear now? She was sick with longing for the sight of his face, and would brave a thousand evil Manitous to gain a single glimpse of his features.

"Be true, be true,
Or thou shalt rue,"

sang a voice in her dream. Why should these words repeat themselves in her mind? She was faithful and true. What sin was she committing? What spirit could work her harm? She reasoned with herself that she only desired to look upon the beloved features which would be reflected in the Clear Water. She now began to assure herself that she had never doubted Wabasso's faithfulness, and that the ear of red corn proved her lover's preference for herself. A good spirit again whispered:

"Turn thee away
From this sin I pray."

"Main-wain-dum-e-yum," said the voice, "it is many years since thy childish prayers were received by the Giver of Life; turn again to that Good which only can sustain thee in this dark hour. The Stream tells the truth no longer, since it is under an evil spell. Pray!" And the echo took up the last word, repeating it again and again till the forest rang with the words, "*Pray! Pray!*" But Ishkodah heeded not the warning. The need of prayer she had never known. *She* had never prayed. She laughed at the thought.

> "She neared the fountain dimly seen
> Before her in the wood;
> An angel laughed, an evil one
> And drove away the good."

As she bent above the crystal basin she heard the croaking laughter of old Guh, and again the voice of Menehwehna warned her to fly from the dreadful place ere it was too late; but she would not heed.

Blinded by the darkness, at first she could see nothing in the pool over which she hung. She waited till her vision cleared, then looked again, but a greater darkness gathered over the heavens and enveloped the forest as if to forbid the act; the winds moaned sullenly among the trees, and the waters cried out against it. Frogs croaked dismally in the shallows, and venomous things hissed in the rank grass. The songs of the birds died away, and in their stead the hoarse cawing of crows came to her ears as they flapped their wings among the branches of the lofty pines; but Ishkodah did not lose courage. The child of a long line of warriors would not yield to fear now, but with face pale as the dead bent above the pool. One look! Her hope was shattered, her faith dead. Despair filled her heart. The threads of her life were broken! Yet she looked again and again upon the fateful vision. What saw she reflected there? She saw Wabasso, the well beloved, whose voice was the sweetest on earth to her, but he was changed. Truthful eye, loving lip, and tuneful voice were no longer for her. She heard him speaking words of love as he knelt before a woman of snow, with hair like shining gold spun into threads to ensnare him. She saw his smile, his gleaming eyes, his voice which told of his love in tones as fond as those to which *she* once had lent a willing ear. The words beat like hail upon her heart.

"By the stars, thou art fair! Give thou thy fairness into mine arms! The gold of thy hair shall be light to mine eyes, and I shall find heaven in the blue of thine!"

His suit was not pressed in vain.

Ishkodah turned to fly from the spot, but awoke to find herself alone at midnight in the forest, to hear again the mocking laugh of old Guh, and feel the terrible fascination of her beadlike eyes. She sunk upon her knees. Her lips moved in hoarse whispers to tell the pain of her heart. "Him only have I loved! I need not many Manitous! With him to guide, what need of spirits great or small? How joyfully I prepared the food brought by his hand for our needed nourishment, or swept the hearth with the fragrant boughs of cedar. How skillfully I dressed the skins with which to furnish our lodge, making them soft as the breast of a dove. I fashioned his garments and the gay coverings for his swift feet. At evening I met him returning from the chase, and when the daylight was quite gone he cheered me with his love to help my courage for the next day's parting. Now all is changed! Another shares the heart which was once mine alone. He brings another love into our lodge. No longer may it be called the 'Wigwam of Peace!' Bitterness will flavor our food since *she* must share it!" Ishkodah's strength failed her at this thought, and she fell to the earth.

"She dies!" screamed the exultant voice of Guh. At a word from her, gaunt forms of the dead gathered around the exhausted girl, and reached out their direful arms to make her their own. In the horrible confusion about her, Ishkodah heard her father's voice: "Unhappy woman! Thy disobedience hath caused thy death! Thou art under the spell of the wicked Guh, and eternal misery awaits thee, unless thou callest upon the Spirit of Good, who holds thy breath, but who even now hath power to save thee!"

At the sound of the familiar and commanding tones, life once more ran in the veins of the dying girl. With an effort she roused her failing faculties, and knowing the terrors of eternity to be near, she cried aloud unto the God whom she had so long forgotten! The hollow eyes of the specters shot fearful flames toward her, but at that Name they drew back and harmed her not. Ishkodah realized now that her strength and safety lay in the name of that Great Spirit whose protection she had not felt the need of until now.

"The Big Sea Water" moaned upon the shore, its gigantic sobbing shook the earth, and Ishkodah knew it to be her funeral dirge. The Master of Life was about to recall the soul he had given, and she had no wish to rebel against His will; but she longed to return to her lodge once more, that she might die amid its simple and familiar furnishings, to leave all memory of the fearful place where she now was behind her. She *prayed* that her strength might last till the daylight came, as none could ever leave the haunted ground in darkness.

"When daylight is upon the earth, then may the children of men walk in safety."

Her father's words! *He* had never had to do with deeds of darkness, but always walked in the light of good deeds.

The rosy streamers of Morning fanned the phantoms from Ishkodah's over-wrought brain. Her fast was at an end. Her eyes were open to the knowledge that in the drink which Guh had given her she had found her death. With wavering and uncertain steps she made her way through the rank grass, to fall among the flowers which grew before the door of her lodge.

A white dove came and perched above the door, and as the soul of her who had made her husband happy, purified by grief and repentance, passed over her lips in a prayer to the Spirit of Good, the bird caught the words in their flight and bore them away to the Receiver of all prayers, whose silver lodge stands on the brink of Death and at the edge of Life:

"Great Michabou, I have sinned! The night of death enfoldeth me. Purify my lodge from the demon of disbelief which sat by its hearth. Life's flame dieth out. The soul of

Ishkodah is like a spark in the ashes. Help thou the weakness of her feet, that she may not stumble in the way of Eternity."

As the dove soared away with the words of the dying girl, the *shadow* of a man appeared at the door of the lodge—a man whose face was like moonlight, whose raiment was transparent as thin clouds, and who, when the body of Ishkodah had been broken by Pauguk (Death), lifted the soul in his shadowy arms and bore it through the mists to the pure realms of the upper air.

In the morning, when the women found that Main-wain-dum-e-yum had left the earth, leaving nothing but a broken shell in the lodge, which they had been wont to call the "Lodge of Peace," they gathered in crowds—old Guh with them—and set out to bear the news to the returning warriors.

Wabasso, more eager than the rest, rode forward to greet them, thinking to see Main-wain-dum-e-yum. She was not there. He hid his disappointment beneath gay words and proudly smiling eyes as he waved the scalps he had won before them. But what means the wailing voices of the squaws? What is the mournful tale they chant?

"Deck not thyself with the bands of wampum and feathers of triumph! Thy gay colors, thy fringes of glory, must be put away; thou must cover thy head with the blanket of grief, for she who once made thee happy is dead!"

The women dared not reveal the cause of Ishkodah's death, fearing to come under the spell of old Guh, who pretended to mourn for the girl as much as any of them.

This was the warrior's welcome home. The scalps and feathers of victory fell from his hands. The horse, from which he had dismounted, finding itself free to join its fellows in the near pasture, whinnied "farewell" to its master as it trotted away. The men hung their heads in sorrow and the women mourned, but *he* uttered no sound of grief, though his life had been robbed of all joy. Where but a moment before the fever of triumph filled his heart, the icy fingers of Death now pressed with benumbing weight. Mournfully he sought his lodge. All was cold and desolate within. No fire burned upon its hearth, the embers were scattered and dead as his hope. The light of his home was gone.

"Where is She of the Silent Tongue? Where is my love, Main-wain-dum-e-yum?"

The white bird heard the cry of the tortured soul, and returned to perch once more upon the poles of the lodge. Death and the wings of Pauguk enveloped him in a garment of ice as he clasped to his broken heart the shell-like thing, which was all that was left of his bride. He laid himself upon the couch, and long did he clasp the shell to his breast, but uttered no sound. The dove waited.

At last his name was softly spoken, in tones which seemed to come from above the trees.

"My faithful one! Thou art guiltless, yet must suffer. Thine unworthy Main-wain-dum-e-yum, grown weary of thine absence, drank of the jealous cup. Fear not, the serpent which crept into thy lodge hath died of its own sting; but the Father of Souls hath heard the cry of my repentance, and hath preserved my soul for thee in the Happy Hunting Grounds."

Joyfully the soul of the warrior escaped its bonds. "Main-wain-dum-e-yum," he whispered, "I come to join thee. Gitchie Manitou, lift up my soul." The dove soared away with the words as he laid the shell-like thing in his breast, and, taking the hand which the Silent Man with the moonlight face and shadowy garments held out to him, they went into the clouds together, bearing the memory of life's mistakes between them, as a help to higher happiness in the Lodge of Eternity.

MEDICINE FEAST.

I ONCE witnessed at the Island of Mackinac the celebration of a Medicine Feast for the cure of the young Indian, Black Beaver, who was the victim of consumption. Black Beaver had, as have all Indians, his superstitions, and had consulted the Medicine Men, or prophets—those who could foretell events—in regard to his case and the chances there were for his cure. A question of such serious import called for more than human knowledge, and no time was lost by the priests in setting forward preparations for solemnly invoking and consulting the spirit of the Great Turtle.

A small lodge was set up inside an enclosure oblong in shape, about one hundred by thirty feet in width. This enclosure had no roof, but its sides were covered with birch bark and dirty pieces of blankets, interspersed occasionally by a clean one, a gay shawl of plaid, or a width of carpet, and all fastened together by long wooden needles or bits of stovepipe wire, and these again secured to a framework of poles or posts.

The Medicine Men, having been warned by a dream, "put on the sacerdotal robes and ministered at the sacred fires"—an old shirt reaching to the knees, a pair of leggings, a belt of wampun and the medicine bag; the fire, a few smouldering brands beside a whisky barrel.

The small tent, or lodge, which had been

put up at the end of the enclosure was formed of some valuable skins, and especial attention was given to the strength of the structure, because of the "workings of the Spirit" when it had once entered the sacred place. By the side of the inner lodge a few odorous pine logs smouldered to exorcise evil spirits. All who were to assist at the celebration assembled at sunset. Nearly the whole population of the village were present as witnesses. The priest approached the small lodge intended for the reception of the Spirit, on his hands and knees; and his head was hardly under its cover before a terrible clap of thunder pealed out of the sky. This seemed to have a direct effect on the mysterious inner wigwam, for it immediately began to tremble and sway from side to side, and "small" voices were distinctly heard calling from a distance; the barking of dogs, the growling of wolves and other animals was also heard for a time, and then suddenly the silence was as complete as the noise had been boisterous.

Two Medicine Men—subordinates of the one in the tent—sat near the fire, smoking long-stemmed pipes of red clay—these were "peace pipes." The first two puffs, with much ceremony and mutterings between, were sent to the East and the West; the next in similar manner were blown toward the North and the South; this signified the presence of the Great Spirit in every place. After the ceremony of the Pipes, the patient was brought into the circle by a couple of braves, as hideously painted as the seriousness of the occasion demanded, who laid the sick man upon the spicy couch of boughs which had been prepared for him; and, poor fellow! this was his death bed. No pillow but the earth, no covering but the sky!

Sitting on their haunches close to the walls of the enclosure, the dancers formed a circle around the patient while awaiting the harangue of the prophet. In his incantation the Medicine Man used the thunder and lightning which occasionally rolled and flashed across the heavens, as a text.

"Behold a mighty spirit, mighty in the air and in the earth, in fire, in water; as mighty by the day as by the night. Oh! thou son of a great chief, if thou art to be cured, the Spirit of the Great Turtle will send his answer in the voice of thunder; but if thou art to die and be numbered with the fallen leaves of the year, a silent flash from heaven shall bear the message."

The dancers sprang to their feet as the priest ceased speaking, and without waiting for the manifestation of the Spirit, they began dancing the celebrated Medicine dance to words something like *hi-ho-hi-e-o*, beating time with hand and foot to the music of the flute, the drum, the rattle, and other rude and noisy instruments. Round and round they danced, uttering, in the intervals of the song, a profusion of unintelligible sounds. The light of the fire showed the decorations of the women to be particularly hideous, some being adorned with old dried scalps, to which a few threads of hair still clung; others wore strings of the small bones of infants about their waists, but the ornaments with which their dresses were decorated were rich and fantastic, and if the filthiness of their persons had not been so great, might have been admired and praised. As it was, one could hardly endure to look upon them, much less admire. Their filthiness beggared description! The men, more dignified in their fringes and embroidery, their belts of wampun and head-dresses of trailing feathers, did the honors—a step in advance of the women, keeping time with their musical instruments to the tinkling bells, or ornaments of silver and brass which their women wore upon wrist and ankle.

The darkness was intense, with no light but that of the flickering fire, and all were in a frenzy of excitement. Never was witnessed a scene more wild and infernal. Never for an instant did the dancing cease. When a dancer, exhausted, threw himself upon the ground, a fresh young squaw or lusty buck sprang into the vacant place, that the dance might continue unbroken to the end of the fourth day.

No sign had yet been sent to the priest by the Spirit of the Turtle, but with the dancing still going on, ceremonies in the way of assisting the Spirit proceeded; the subordinates employed outside the sacred lodge each did his share toward ameliorating the sick man's sufferings; each in turn approached the patient, and placing two or three bead-like pellets between his lips, pressed the body forward until the head touched the knees; then, with a swift push backward, laid him once more prostrate.

The relatives and friends outside the "charmed circle" were making offerings, fasts and penances, and dreadful tests of endurance to propitiate the god whom they had invoked; and no one seemed to receive injury from the performances unless we except Black Beaver, who, when at last a flash of lightning proclaimed his doom, and the "wee small voice" of the Spirit, supposed to be in communication with the Medicine Man, uttered the words: "The course of the youth is run; he must die;" was already more dead than alive.

This feast was celebrated with less than the usual ceremony because of the situation and unsuitable surroundings; the nearness of residences and the noises of the town where should have been the silence of the forest. It was a great relief to those who witnessed the ceremony, when the soul of Black Beaver had sped upon its swift journey, and his body carried away from the place.

Coffined in a rude basket of birch bark, made waterproof by the application of resin and pitch, the body of the dead chief was deposited in a magnificent canoe, and amid chantings and beating of drums, followed by a long procession of water craft, each crowded to its utmost capacity by hideously painted men and mourning women, was paddled across the Straits to the Indian burial ground on Round Island, and there laid to rest.

CORN DANCE.

THE origin of corn has been something of a puzzle, but the conclusion from all evidence is, that it first grew in the highlands of Mexico. It was cultivated by the Indians of that region, and from them spread, so that by the time Columbus arrived it was known and used nearly everywhere on the continent. The Indians claim to have received the seed direct from the Great Spirit.

The earliest species is described as having each kernel enclosed in a separate husk like grains of wheat in the head. The varieties are now almost beyond account, the Indians having produced such well-defined mixtures of kernels on the ears as to make it possible to determine by what tribe any ear was grown. For example, one tribe has all red and white ears, another all black, and so on, even to the arrangement of the different colored grains on the ear. These distinctions are said to have been adopted for the purpose of detecting thefts of corn by one tribe from another.

The Corn Dance was celebrated when the crops were especially bountiful as a thank-offering to the Great Spirit for having supplied them with food in plenty. Corn was the name applied by *our* Indians to food of any kind, whether "fish, flesh, or fowl." The dance was supposed to be performed annually at the time of the payment to the Indians of their annuities by the Government. If it

THE DANCERS.

chanced that the paymaster was prevented, by stress of weather or other reason, from making his rounds at the usual time, or if the traders had a claim on the money due poor "Lo" and his brothers—they having "eaten it up" or its value before receiving it—the feast was removed and celebrated on the *arrival* of the paymaster, or at such time as the *circumstances* of the Indians permitted.

The musical instruments usually employed at these celebrations were the common drum or tom-tom—three in number—and the simple five-hole flute; the drums highly decorated with quills, beads, bells, and coins; the quills representing industry, the bells for exorcising evil spirits, and the coins signifying power. The drummers sat some distance apart to admit of a circle of singing braves and squaws being formed around each, while a line of fifty or more warriors, each with gaily-ornamented sticks with which to beat time to the music, formed an outer circle around them, the flute player standing alone and at some distance, piping the dismal measure, which with the tom-tom accompanied the weird singing of men and women. At the first note of the flute a chosen leader begins a fantastic dance around and in and out among the inner circles, after which he pauses to make his thank-offering to the Great Spirit for the benefits he has received. During his harangue the warriors of the outer circle dance a monotonous step, and not until each one has given thanks do they cease from the performance.

The second chosen dancer varies not in the least from the manner of the first; the singing is the same, the dancing of the outer circle during his speech is the same, and thus the ceremony proceeds until all have given thanks. Four days is the time usually occupied in the celebration of the Corn Dance.

GHOST DANCE.

THE days of Indian Summer were usually devoted to the annual games and thank-offerings of the Indians, which young men and old, women and maidens, toddling babes and well-swaddled papooses, gathered to engage in or witness, each brilliant with additional paint and plumage, and lending the touch of color which gay blankets and bright embroideries alone can produce, and all eager to see the prizes secured by their favorites.

The racing, climbing, leaping, and wrestling matches were over and the prizes about to be awarded, when a ferocious grizzly bear invaded the space set apart for the sports, to be fought and killed by young To-wah-bic, who had already won *the white feather* for the most difficult climbing, to which was added a fine string of *wampum* beads as a tribute to his bravery and skill in the dispatch of Bear. This compliment so inflamed his zeal and pride that he determined to enter the swimming contest, to win, if possible, the royal canoe which was offered as a prize.

Michibou thus far had smiled upon the efforts of To-wah-bic, but as the day wore on the Manitou repented of his partiality, and, deeming the avaricious disposition exhibited by the youth as unworthy of a brave, determined on his punishment. He frowned upon the young man, and resolved upon his death.

As To-wah-bic with the other contestants struck out for the stake to which the valuable prize was secured, the voice of the angry god was heard ordering in thunder tones his blackest and most forbidding clouds to hide the descending sun, while the lightning terrors of his eyes flashed through the scudding clouds, sending all but two of the terrified swimmers back to the safety of the shallows.

By the lurid gleams of the lightning the two determined ones were seen breasting the breakers, and, spurred by fear, making frantic efforts to reach the canoe, which Mah-nah-be-zee laid hold of as To-wah-bic fell back into the clutches of the god, who had entered the water in the shape of a monstrous sturgeon to seize him. The women sang a death song, and called upon the medicine men to quell the storm and save him if they could.

Sacrificial fires were quickly kindled, offerings made, and the mercy of the gods invoked, but without avail. To-wah-bic's doom was sealed, and as Mah-nah-be-zee, exhausted by his battle with the waves, was hauled over the side of the hardly-won prize, the doomed youth sank beneath the waves.

The gay day ended in clouds and tears; the happy hearts were sad; the games were declared closed, and the Corn Dance, which was to have finished the celebration, was deferred because of the anger of the gods.

The winds sighed themselves to sleep; the crested waves smoothed themselves out to reflect the glances of the stars, which peered now and again from behind the heaps of clouds which rolled across the heavens in their haste to leave the hateful scene. Chibi-ah-bos set the water spirits to their pulsing musical tasks; mothers breathed or hummed "songs without words" to soothe their restless babes; Mishinauwa brought the pipes and noiselessly distributed them among the smokers, who lingered with the sad-hearted throng near the scene of the disaster, to hear the interpretation of the Prophet.

A luminous light spread over the earth, showing that the moon was not far off, and the flames flickered fitfully upon the crisp cinders of the recent offerings of propitiation. Swarthy features and dark eyes gleamed in the firelight. Blue flannel shirts softly faded into gray. Fringed leggings and heavily-draped blankets mingled with the gay shawls of the women and blended with the bright bands of red which stretched along the western sky.

The squaws, swathed in soft cottons, their full throats and dark heads bare to the kisses of the night, tended their papooses, or noiselessly played with the toddling warriors in embryo, whose little cries of petulance or joy —babbling noises from throats that would not always be musical, no sooner uttered than hushed—made a picture never to be forgotten —the color of Italy in northern Michigan.

At last the musical silence was broken, and the voice of the Prophet floated to the listening ears: "In my dreams I have seen that the Pale Face who has landed on our shores bodes the Indian no good. His great canoe, whose sails are clouds, breathes fire and smoke to consume us. He comes to take from us our homes and our lands. By the venom of a stinging bee I have been warned that the Red Man must soon leave the land of his fathers. Every breeze whispers of the stranger who brings destruction to our race. Our gods are against us—we know not how to appease their anger—the skies are streaked with blood; To-wah-bic is gone, and every sign speaks of death! Look! the god drags him down! His manliness and beauty lost forever!"

Stirred by the Meda's unusual excitement, the men and women hurried to the shore; but they were powerless to help the ghastly shape which floated here and there in the clutches of the tremendous fish. Myriads of spirits crowded upon the bosom of the lake to witness the dance of death, adding their weird and mysterious noises to the terrors of the scene.

Horror-stricken, the people watched the host of ghost-like shapes take place upon the curling waves to perform the Death Dance. Pale phosphorescent lights illumined the water; the stars fled, and terrified curs slunk whining behind the nearest wigwam curtain; frightened cries of children were hushed by those who trembled and grew faint in turn, while wolves snarled in the near forest, a fit accompaniment to the unearthly performance.

Round and round in circles, varied by the measure of the weird music, whirled To-wah-bic, fast gripped in the arms of the Manitou, whom wonderful spiral streams lifted to the heavens to dash again into the deeps, while the phantoms and specters of the dead encircled them on every side, and with the whole spirit population joined in a great revolving whirl of evolution, which all the gods drew near to witness.

Suddenly the moon appeared, her pale and unearthly light a sign of doom. Beneath her cold glance To-wah-bic and the sturgeon sunk with lightning speed; the specters melted into thin air; gods and Manitous resumed their earthly shapes; the fairies flew away, and the suddenly depopulated waves beat sweet and limpid measures as they lapped upon the sands.

Again the Prophet spoke: "In this dread scene I clearly read our doom; like shapes of mist our race will pass away to be no more remembered."

The prophecy is nearing its fulfillment. Of Hiawatha's thirteen nations ten are gone, and soon this once powerful people will have disappeared forever.

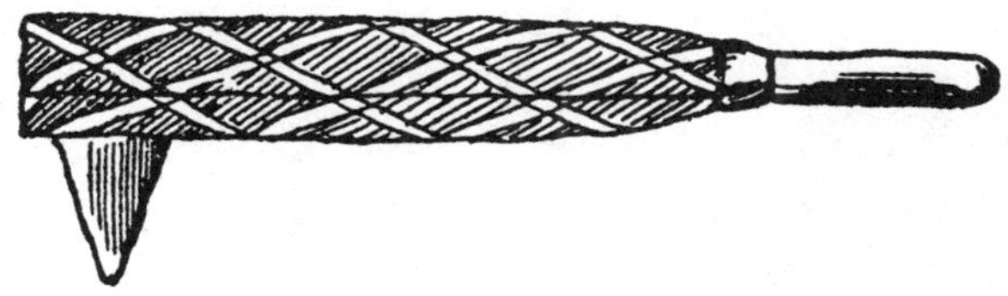

WHITE CHRISTIAN AND BLUE INDIAN.

THE young wife of old Tuskenow awoke from an uneasy slumber. There was a great rushing of the wind gods across the heavens, through the forest and over the great black lake. She shivered with dread, for in spite of her wish to be rid of them, and to be as her teacher, the White Christian, the superstitions, traditions, and beliefs of her race had still a strong hold upon her mind, though she was beginning to receive and believe the teachings of Christianity.

The storm raged furiously as she raised the curtain of her lodge and looked out into the night. Near the horizon the heavens wore the gray of approaching dawn, where she could see a great flock of wild geese flying obliquely across them. A soul was freeing itself from the trammels of earth, her old beliefs told her.

A flock of plovers flying in a curved line toward the south stopped to rest on the birchen poles of her wigwam. From them she gathered that the soul had escaped, and was now resting from its laborious transit from the earth.

She thought of the White Christian whom her people had named the *Black Coat;* he had told her of the beautiful Garden of Paradise which corresponded with the Happy Hunting Grounds of the Indian, and she wondered if her old husband had left her lodge fire to enjoy a better and more comfortable life in that great Garden, the home of all pure souls, and heavenly birds, and all creatures who do the will of that Great Spirit who cares for all. She longed to be free, and to go to the sacred place where the souls of the dead live forever, where game was always plenty, where no famine could come, no wars disturb, but where all was peace.

She longed to trust the White Christian, and would gladly have given her sick husband into his care, but her people would not allow it. They had taken the sick chief from his lodge, and were already celebrating a medicine feast for the restoration of his health; but if the birds told truly, Tuskenow was no longer living. She had a secret hope that the White Christian would have assisted her to prevent the celebration of the feast. Alone, she was powerless. But the White Christian had not forbidden it, and the rites were performed as usual. Indeed, the priest was as powerless as herself; and seeing that the old man was about to die, he said nothing.

While she was yet standing at the door of her lodge, Newebozho, the friend and lover of her youth, drew near to inform her that the feast had failed, that the offerings were rejected; this was the interpretation of the Medicine Men, and Tuskenow had already passed to the Place of Souls.

The young Noko (wife) bowed her head in the ashen folds of her blanket, but uttered no sound of grief nor gave way to mourning. Tuskenow was old and ready for the pleasures of the Happy Hunting Grounds, where he had believed himself to be going; and though she had respected him and served him faithfully, she had not loved him, and could not mourn for him as other women mourned.

She much desired to comply with the oft-repeated wish of her husband to lay his body within the sacred caverns of the Great Turtle, especially as he had expressed a fear that unless this was done, his spirit would be delayed on its journey to the plenteous fields of the Future Life.

Noko knew that the way to those mysterious caverns had been lost for many generations, and that none of the wise men or prophets had been able to reveal it. Noko was still young. Her old husband was also her chief, and though she had not given her heart to him when she had joined hands with him, she revered his memory and hoped for his future happiness. She did not *now* believe that his burial within the subterranean caves of the island would in the least influence the Master of Life to reward Tuskenow more than he would otherwise be rewarded if laid to rest in the common burial-place of his people; but her husband believed and she had once believed in these things, and therefore determined to carry out, if possible, the wishes of the aged man.

Newebozho waited in silence at the lodge door of the young widow. He had loved her in the days of his youth—he loved her still. In those bygone days they had been plighted lovers. He had gone upon the war-path, and, returning, found the beloved one already wedded to another.

No excuses on her side, no reproaches on his. The girl's guardians said that as he was a Blue Indian he could not legitimately marry one of their race. His parentage and his birthplace were unknown to them, they repeatedly informed him; and as he had no knowledge of them himself, this was not to be wondered at.

The thoughts of Newebozho flew back to the time of his great disappointment, when he had accepted his fate with what courage he could command; he remembered how he had determined to trace his lineage, and, if possible, remove the reproach cast upon his birth. In his dreams he had succeeded in doing so, though never quite *clearly;* but as he stood thus waiting beside the lodge of his early and only love, the way seemed open to him. A great hope filled his heart; but he kept his eyes upon the ground, fearing to give her the *glance of love* so soon after the death of her husband.

Her head was now uncovered in the faint light of the dawn, and with tearful eyes fixed upon the fast flying clouds, Noko began to speak. Joy rang bells in *his* heart at the sound of the well-beloved voice, though each pleasing recollection, every kind word or generous action of the dead man rose in *her* mind and brought regretful tears.

"Tuskenow is dead. No more will he chant his prayers to the Sun, which to him was the eye of the Great Spirit. He is dead, and I weep for him!" She calmed herself, and after a time continued:

"I could wish, good Newebozho, to lay him to rest among the ancient and mysterious people of the underground paths. The way to these caverns has been hidden for ages. Who shall discover it for me? How quiet would be his rest in so secret a bed—his war-knives, his bows and arrows, his pipes and vermilion, his belt of the sacred wampum, and the feathers of Victory ready for his use and need in the world to which he has gone! Our people fear these dark places of the dead, but Tuskenow feared them not, nor do I fear to fulfill his wish to sleep there." She hesitated: "If the White Christian, who is known to be very wise and patient, could be induced to lend his aid, it might help me to the performance of this last sacred duty to my chief."

A chill of ice shook the very centers of Newebozho's being when his beloved Noko suggested asking the advice of the "Black Coat." His peculiar bluish complexion paled to a grayish hue, and for a moment he was unable to speak. A terrible and relentless hatred for the priest, who was but yesterday his friend, filled his heart. Noko, who was alive to every change of her lover's countenance, reading his thought, exclaimed: "Newebozho is silent! *He dare not* give me his aid! Will he then prevent another doing that which he fears to do himself?"

"Noko is wrong!" muttered the jealous lover. "I alone know the way to the caverns beneath our feet—the ancient burial-place of an extinct race. *I*, born of the blue-clay-earth by a thunderbolt, am its last and only representative. My dreams have revealed the mysterious caves to me, and I shall soon prove myself the legitimate son of the earth and air, with an ancestry as ancient as the world itself; and by the soul of the bravest warriors in those silent depths, I will do as Noko wishes—I will reveal the way!"

Noko, ashamed of her outburst, would have thanked him, but he gently checked her. "Nay, thou shalt not! I love thee! To fail in this is to lose thee, the bright star of my life! Look! Already they bear the body of thy husband to his burial; when the four days of fasting are done, *I* shall be ready. At the darkest hour of the fourth night, when the lights on the old man's grave have burned themselves out, I shall uncover it and bear his body secretly to the foot of the great pine tree which grows near the Red Clay Hill. Meet me at this place, and thine eyes shall see his cherished wish fulfilled. I shall go down into the grave of my long-silent people, bearing thy husband to his last bed among them. Courtesy permits him to lie there, not the right of inheritance, since *his* people are of the New *Last*, and mine of the Old *First* earth!"

Noko, reassured by his promises, thanked him, and when he left her gave no thought to his revelations in regard to his ancestry; for she knew that she loved him for himself, and not for his fathers before him.

At the darkest hour of the fourth night of

the festival of the dead she repaired to the Red Clay Hill to witness the burial of her husband in the interior of the revered Great Turtle. Her keen eyes pierced the darkness which enveloped her on every hand, and she soon made out the form of Tuskenow where it lay upon the ground at the foot of the pine tree, but as yet Newebozho was not visible.

Pale moonlit shadows played upon the calm features of 'the dead chief, and Noko felt that he was greatful to her; that she was obeying the call of duty, and hoped from the depths of her pure heart that the good old man might sleep well. These thoughts comforted her, for the night pressed upon her as of dark portent.

The cry of the loon came mournfully to her from across the lake; an owl on silent wing flew over her head, and birds of evil omen hovered near. With a whispered prayer for help, she crossed herself as she had seen the White Christian do, and named the One Name. At this act of reverent faith the odorous night flowers seemed to breathe those words of the White Christian's faith upon the still air: "Evil is overcome by faith in Christ." It was as if the midnight woodland were a lofty and holy church, consecrated to the wonderful Son of the Great Father of whom the White Christian had told them. The Four Brothers—the Winds—sang a requiem for the dead, and she was there as a mourner. The flowers sent up their ambrosial incense, and through it all rang again and again those other words which the White

Christian had used in his missions among them: "A light to them that sit in darkness and in the shadow of death, to guide their feet into the way of peace."

A great longing to *be* a Christian now filled her soul. This undertaking once over, she would speak her faith in these teachings; and could she but influence Newebozho to do so, they might at last be happy. She was now in great haste to have her sad errand over, that she might seek the priest and tell him of her wish to have his God for her God, of her wish to accept the Christ in place of the many Manitous which she had hitherto believed in and worshiped. The Word, which is all powerful to create, was working in young Noko's heart.

But what detained Newebozho? Noko's eyes sought the ground at the thought of her lover, and as she had hoped, soon saw him rising through a fissure in the rocks, his finger upon his lip, enjoining silence as he stooped to lift the stiffened form of the old chief from the ground. Noko followed as he raised the burden of clay to his powerful shoulders and disappeared again within the trembling earth, from which he had just emerged. Noko fearlessly felt her way through the slimy crevices of the downward path until the light which went before was clearer and more steady, and at last became fixed. They made their way by narrow and difficult paths into broad and stately halls and corridors until they stood within the great Cave of the Dead, which she had so much desired to find. The wonders of the nether world stretched out before her sight. Vast arches of amethyst and crystal upheld mighty walls encrusted with brilliants of every rainbow hue.

A deep voice thus greeted their entrance: "Welcome, thou child of the Earth and Air; and welcome thou, daughter of the Day! The Sun no longer warms the clay of that burden which ye bear to its rest among the sacred dead. Ages have rolled away since these paths have echoed to the tread of living feet! Yet are ye welcome! Lay thy burden in my breast and hasten again into the sunlight. All is well. Dead heroes sleep well when they have passed through the fearful but holy valley to reach the mountain of perfection."

Newebozho placed the body of Tuskenow upon a ledge of rock near which a clear stream trickled. The place was cold and gruesome in spite of its jeweled grandeur, and Noko was glad to leave it, guided by the friend who had so well fulfilled his promises. The Voice of the Cave seemed strangely familiar; its tones were like Newebozho's and constantly recurred to her, though they could not drown those which she had heard at Red Clay Hill, "A light to them that sit in darkness."

Morning was abroad upon the waters, though the forest was still enveloped in shadows, when they emerged from the heart of the earth through a small opening or archway beneath the dog god which lies at the feet of those godlike lovers,* towering above it in mighty grandeur. Surprised, Noko said:

---

* Three Manitous.

"Why hast thou brought me to the feet of the three most sacred Manitous of my people? My lodge is distant, and I am weary."

"This way have we traversed that thou mightst see the graven body of my *first* mother. My dreams have revealed the sepulchre of the first woman of the world, the mother of my race. My father is the aged keeper of the Place of Souls. His voice recalled to thee my own." As he spoke Newebozho loosened with his foot a boulder in the hillside, and placed it to one side, disclosing as he did so an opening in the cliff where sat the perfect body of a woman, whose flesh was of the same peculiar color and as life-like in appearance as that of Newebozho's own, whose ancestors had owed their origin to her. Lying beside her, in this long-hidden grave, were many curious implements and pictured histories of a long-buried people.

As Noko gazed with frightened but believing eyes upon this long-forgotten woman of the world, she admitted that Newebozho had spoken truly of his ancestry, and that his lineage was ancient before her own race existed.

"Forgive me," she whispered, and Newebozho's heart relented toward the love of his youth, though he understood from her manner that she had heretofore looked upon him as her inferior, and for that reason, in spite of the pledges of faith and love given him, had wedded the old man whom they had just laid in the grave.

"How is it with thee, my Noko?" he asked

gently. "Have I unearthed this witness of the past for naught? My first mother will now crumble into dust like a sigh of the breeze, and there will be no more trace of my people. Our histories shall become as tattered rags of an old superstition, and our implements will be called thunderbolts by which men may die! Can the Black Coat show thee more than this?"

Tears stood in Noko's eyes as she answered:

"Dear Newebozho, thy worth is more than proved. By this," pointing to the now fast crumbling blue woman, "and by the relics enclosed in her grave, thou hast proved that thy people once possessed the land of my fathers! The White Christian hath showed me the way of truth by which the souls of all men may live! The test of worth is the same as the test of truth—I love thee!" The pain in his longing eyes made her admit this: "I love thee! and oh, as thou lovest me, name *the* Name and *believe*, that we at last may find happiness!"

The dark features of Newebozho underwent a change. "Let me think on thy words," he said; "if I shall name *the* Name, *we* shall be happy," repeating the words, "*we shall be happy*" again and again.

"Name the Name and *believe*," repeated the agitated girl, whose heart beat with hope as she saw the look of hatred and jealousy fade from her lover's countenance. There was no cure for that malady in the history of her people, but she hoped that the cross of the White Christian might miraculously purify his heart, and if this was accomplished she would gladly give to Newebozho the vacant seat in her lodge. She hoped that what human love had failed in, the Cross would perform. As these thoughts of faith and hope and love flashed in her mind, Noko plucked and bound together two branches in the shape of a cross, and gently laid it against her lover's breast. Her heart, great with love, smiled upon him through her tear-dimmed eyes; she loved him and wished to save him to enjoy with her an eternal life beyond the grave. She felt that unless the mysterious Cross could save him, he was lost to her and to all joy forever.

She would not leave him with his heart in pain, so, taking his hand, she urged him to go with her to the "lodge of peace," in which the White Christian dwelt. "Come, let us seek him," she said; "he will give us life from a great tree whose sap cures all ills. His understanding is greater than that of our wise men. Come, let us go to him."

The branches of the little cross in Newebozho's bosom seemed to burst into bloom as the words, "Thy faith hath saved thee," vibrated melodiously on the air. Noko caught them to her as she leaned upon his breast. The cross had saved him, and he felt it, as he clasped the loving woman to him. He heard the words, "Go and sin no more," and turning saw the White Christian near them in the woods, a crucifix uplifted in his hands, as though he blessed them.

The priest knew of the early love of these two hearts, its unhappy termination, their miserable parting. Newebozho confessed his jealous fault. The White Christian censured, but forgave and blessed him. Together the lovers knelt to receive his benediction.

There was strength and refreshment in the act, and no trifling power in the earnest words of faith and Christian love spoken by the man of God, whose inmost heart yearned to lead these poor lost children of the forest into the way of life. The dew of mercy fell upon them, and they were once more happy. Once more they covered the grave of the first mother of Newebozho's Jovian race, and after sealing it with wet clay and gravel, took their way through the woods in the direction of the village, accompanied by the White Christian, who gave them wise counsel in regard to their future movements, infusing their hearts, at the same time, with a courage hitherto unknown to them.

Though weary from the night's exertions, they were happy, and fear was far from them; yet danger lurked in the forest, and death was before them. They had been followed, and where the wood was thickest were surrounded by a constantly-increasing horde of blue spirits, who attacked them with invincible implements (thunderbolts), at the same time crying out to the priest, "Thou hast taken from us our Son! The last of our race! The last son of the first of earth's people! Give up! give up our son!"

Clinging to each other in great fear, Noko and Newebozho kept as near to the White Christian as the dense and thickly-growing brush and brambles would permit, and continued to press onward, with the Cross always before them as an emblem of peace and goodwill both to the quick and the dead, until at last the path became so entangled that they were forced to stay their steps.

The blue spirits fell upon them and wounded them almost to death. Rocks were torn open and the forest growth of ages crashed upon them, so that the White Christian, at last overpowered, let the Cross fall from his hands and sank upon his knees. Newebozho's faith wavered. He feared that the Cross had lost its power.

"These are the jealous spirits of my dead," he whispered. "Let me give the White Christian the Cross which thou gavest me, lest the blue spirits destroy him. I would save the life of this good man!"

"No—no! Let not go thy hold upon the Cross;" and Noko, grasping the staff from his hand crossed it over her own and leaped with it to the side of the White Christian as he fell to the ground. Fasting and the hardships of the forests had so weakened the priest that, though he fought bravely to protect himself and the young couple from the contending elements, he at last sank dying beneath the crushing weight of a giant forest tree.

Noko threw herself upon the ground beside him, and as he breathed his last the spirits of the air laughed and mocked at her; and had not the Cross been so closely fixed in the breast of Newebozho, he would soon have yielded to those blue spirits of jealousy, and thus lost *eternally* the woman whom he so long had loved. Valiantly he fought against the fiends who tortured him, and when at last he too fell at the feet of the faithful Noko, and the spirits tore from his breast the "outward symbol of an inward grace," his spirit had already fled to join that of the White Christian in the fields of peace.

The unhappy Noko threw herself upon one and then upon the other. She brought water in her hands and sprinkled upon them, but they were dead, and she could not rouse them; and if the teachings of the White Christian were true, their souls were alive now in the Garden of Paradise, where she hoped soon to join them. When the Spirits of the storm had subsided, she began to dig a grave for them, lest their dear bodies be torn by the wild beasts of the forest. She had nothing but the branch of a tree with which to remove the earth, and her tender hands were torn and bleeding before her task was done. She washed the faces of these dear ones whom she was to see no more in this life, and laid them in the shallow bed which she had made. With loose earth and fragrant leaves she covered them, and rolled down upon them the heaviest stones and boulders she could find, that they might sleep undisturbed. When she had made a fresh cross, and in the name of Christ placed it upon the double grave, the labor of love, which had taken the whole day to accomplish, was done, and the weary woman took her way through the misty evening shadows to her lonely lodge. Her faith was strong, and her mind at rest concerning her future. Her baptism had been as by fire, her consecration perfect.

That night the blue spirits raged once more 'mid driving rains upon the shoulders of the Great Turtle; and while Noko lay upon her couch listening to the blasts of the storm, the gods of her youthful ignorance closed in, and assisted by dead warriors of the past, fought their last battle for place in her heart; but when morning came *peace* brooded there. The customs and beliefs of her youth trembled and fell from their hitherto high place in her estimation. She had no longer "a thousand thousand gods" to worship nor to fear; the terrible conflict of the night had but fixed her faith and given to her one God alone, whose goodness and power she believed to be invincible. The Christian faith prevailed. Christ had won. Weariness fled before the thought, and her rest was sweet. She seemed to be floating in mid-air. Sweetest music greeted her. She slept; and, in her dream of heaven, was wafted through its gates.

Though all unmarked, the grave of this pure and loving heart, the fields of gold and white daisies, and the delicate blue-bells which spring from the graves of the White Christian and the Blue Indian, are a perpetual reminder of the patient and faithful woman who won her lover from the demons of darkness and superstition and brought him with herself into the strong light of Christianity.

[NOTE.—Some years ago there was discovered in a small cave near the "Giant's Stairway" the body of a woman in a sitting position. The body was in a good state of preservation, and of a peculiar bluish-gray tint, having no doubt taken on the color of the blue clay—a vein of which ran through the cave. On being exposed to the air, the flesh soon crumbled to dust. The bones were collected and kept for some time in one of the cellars of the Mission House and then buried.]

THE HAUNTED WINDOW.

YOUNG AGEMAW, a Chippeway Indian, fell in love with a white girl, whose father, a member of the Fur Company, resided in one of the best – perhaps the best—house in the village of Mackinac. Agemaw was a great brave. When on the war-path, no man was more bloodthirsty or active in securing scalps; he left not a single lock by which his enemies might be drawn up to heaven; but with women, and especially the white maiden who "sat behind glass," whom he loved as only the Indian loves his wife, he was more gentle and considerate than was the usual custom of his people.

The Fur Company man objected to his daughter marrying an "*Injun;*" but the lovers managed to spend many stolen hours together, notwithstanding. The maiden responded to Agemaw's love, and was quick to acquire the ways of the tent-dwellers and roamers of the forest, and learned many things known only to savage life from his teachings.

Her lover taught her to tell the hours of the day by the moving sun, and those of the night by the stars. By his aid flowers grew from her breath. Agemaw was expert at this work, but the white girl could only bring forth two flowers in perfection—the white-leaved lily with a golden heart, which grew upon water, and a wonderful snowy bloom which took the shape of a *pipe*, with its long curving stem and swelling bowl. These, the lover told her, emanated from a pure heart and peaceful mind. Again, the youth taught her to make music, after the Indian fashion, upon a bone flute with *five* perforations—these were love notes—and from it she drew such music as the Indian loves, and with which he wooes the woman whom he would make his wife. He fashioned for her use a tambourine, with silver bells; a rattle of deer's hoofs, tipped with copper—in its handle a note of call for his ear alone; but, most precious of all, he gave into her keeping a magical flower, which opened its petals only at the hour set for their meetings. This blossom had twelve leaves; and if a step were heard on the gravel path which ran before her father's house, the maiden knew if it were her lover's by the turning back of the leaves. Every time Agemaw approached, the flower turned back just so many petals as numbered the hour, but remained tightly closed if any one else came near. Thus it was an easy matter for the young couple to circumvent the designs of those who wished to part them.

The girl was kept a prisoner in a second-story bedroom, the window of which overlooked the beach and western lake, and made access to it easy. With the clock flower to announce his visits, and a light ladder to climb upon the window ledge, young Agemaw was enabled to gain many a delightful interview undetected.

Once, when friendly mists covered the earth and the lake lay shrouded in a thick fog, the flower clock opened its perfumed petals as the ardent lover sought the window to inform his betrothed that he had made plans for their escape the next night.

All went well with them until the night of their intended elopement, when the Moon—that patroness of love and marriage, whom the Indians ever trust—drove away the friendly mists which were aiding the lovers to keep things shady, and threw the broad light of her great lantern upon the western wall of the Fur Company man's house and over the lofty casement, to expose the swarthy Romeo perched there, his long legs dangling from the window sill, his arms encircling the waist of the fair Juliet, as he whispered of his love and hopes for their happiness after they had made their escape. But they had not counted on the variable disposition of the Moon.

The Moon, whom the young couple had believed to be their friend, changed. There is no placing any dependence on the Moon. She has changed before, and will change again.

One of the Moon's daughters had set her heart upon having Agemaw for a husband; and the pale mother—though ashamed of her treachery, and ready to weep at the thought of the life she would lead in case of her failure to give her unruly daughter the man she loved—came out and revealed all that was going on to the Fur Company man—the engagement, the secret meetings, the bold plan of the savage suitor to marry his daughter in spite of opposition.

The Fur Company man saw, with the

Moon's aid, the young Indian slipping down the ladder with the daughter, whom *he* supposed to be safe from what *he* called harm, following lightly after him, and determined to put an end to the "Injun" at once.

The departing pair, all unconscious of the near danger, reached the shore in safety, and were about to push off from it in the canoe which Agemaw had provisioned for their journey, when the Moon, followed by the Fur Company man, with a band of hunters at his back, came upon the scene, and spitefully turned back the folds of her gray cloud blanket to let the light of her lantern stream over their hiding place and prevent their escape.

Overpowered by numbers, the lovers were separated, the fainting girl conveyed to the great house, and the unfortunate Agemaw, unequal to a struggle of ten to one, was soon bound and thrown into the lake. The dreadful whirlpool of the Straits, which had served to cover many a dark deed, swallowed the helpless youth from sight forever; and except that the Moon grew colder in appearance, and often showed signs of tears, things went on as if the youth had never existed, and indeed no unusual thing had occurred. It was no uncommon thing in those days for *those in power* to have a man's scalp, and his body roasting in the parlor stove before breakfast in the morning. But to the maiden, who learned from a chattering neighbor the terrible deed which her father had caused to be committed, it meant much. She accused him of his treachery, placed the guilt of Agemaw's death at his door, and vowed that she would never leave the room where she had been imprisoned nor move from the window where she so often had admitted her lover.

That vow she never broke.

For years the Moon looked coldly upon her as she sat at the casement waiting for the time when she could be called to join her betrothed in the spirit world; but the Sun, as if moved by the sight of her grief, and pleased that a woman had once more proved faithful, came each day with his pencils to paint her likeness on the glasses of the many-paned window near which she sat. On every pane of that old casement the features of the faithful girl may still be seen—an indelible reminder of woman's love and constancy.

After his daughter's death, the Fur Company man repented of his murderous act and joined the church. He was even heard to say that "poor Agemaw was *a good Indian*," though he had not found it out until the poor fellow was *a dead Indian*.

[NOTE.—The glass on which the features of the unhappy girl were most clearly depicted is said to be in the possession of Mrs. John S. Newbury, of Detroit.]

THE GIANT FAIRIES.

TRADITION has it that Mackinac Island, the now famous watering place, was once the home of the Giant Fairies, and that the sloping land at present occupied by the Mission House—which latter is the most interesting of old places—was the frequent rendezvous of the wonderful Indian giants.

The meadow, or flat, near the lake, dotted numerously by deserted muskrat hills and tufts of coarse grass and rushes, is always green and fertile when elsewhere the sod is parched and dry; which is said to be due to the fact that the Giant Fairies did their dancing there—the touch of their feet breaking down the muskrat huts and making the place as green and " blooming as the rose."

How delightful to tell, not of those tiny elves of our childish fancies, but of great creatures thrice the size of our ordinary man. The old-time wee things *might* have been wafted to the island on Zephyr's wings, or on clouds of rainbow mist; but what mighty gales hurled the Giant Geebis to its shores?

The moon was full, and shone upon the sloping green which stretched before the old Mission House, whose great wings were connected by the wide porch in which Scholasticus, a mortal, sat drinking a glass of rarely good wine. The night was fine. No sound broke the stillness save the plashing of the moon-bathed wavelets as they ran sparkling up the beach.

Singly, or in groups of two and three, the Indians left the agency and sauntered through the Mission grounds on their way to the smoky couches which awaited them in the wigwams, which were pitched, as usual, on the hill-top, back of the "Black Coat's" house.

One by one their fires went out; one by one the lights in the village disappeared; and Scholasticus was draining his last glass and thinking of bed himself, when he saw a cloud of flame moving toward the meadow, lapping and crowding upon each other like unruly sheep. As they continued to advance, he soon made out that the flames were enormous *fireflies* swarming toward the flat near the lake; while before them—like a drum-major with his baton—walked the biggest man the scholastic mortal ever saw, and as dainty on a gigantic scale as were ever the old-time sprites of his childhood imaginings. The creature was *graceful*, too, and *twenty feet high*, and on his head he wore a cap of flowers. His dress was a gigantic tiger-lily put on topsy-turvy. and his *wand* was a young sapling as long as the giant was tall. With this he distributed the fireflies about the turfy banks of the Muskrat Hills, till the whole place seemed to be hung with enormous electric lamps, each one larger and more powerful than the largest moon.

The water, as smooth as glass, reflected the lights, and made the most delicious melody as it softly washed upon the gravely beach—finer than was ever heard by mortal before; and, as an accompaniment, every blue-bell growing in the sloping fields—suddenly grown large and turned to silver—rang out a peal of marvelous and delightful sound. A tent flower of great size and delicate coloring rose from the top of the largest muskrat hut, and grew and grew until it covered the mushroom stools which sprung up under the direction of the Giant Chamberlain. Fresh swarms of fireflies edged the tent with various colored lights in patterns and devices of their own designing; and when all was finished to the satisfaction of the Chamberlain, he sat down upon a mushroom stool and viewed the arrangements with great complacency.

Soon from every direction troops of Giant Fairies came upon the green, all oddly dressed, and all behaving as those bygone elfin mites behaved, only on a *larger* plan. Their garments were fantastic beyond description. One of the leading belles carried a great fan of butterflies' wings, and wore plumes from the paradise bird ten yards long. A petticoat, made of the skin of a mastodon mole, and worn by the biggest sylph, was greatly admired. One dress was trimmed with rows of ribbon grass a half yard in width, and the number of yards in length hardly to be figured on; added to this, the spread tails of great peacocks fastened upon the shoulders with ornaments to match.

The men were the most absurdly dressed. One wore an old windmill on his head, which, Scholasticus thought, gave him the look of a chief; and another with a blanket of vampires' wings thrown across his shoulders, and a vulture in his hat, resembled a colossal Mercury. Not till Scholasticus saw the Giant Chamberlain conduct each one to his seat, did he realize that he was witnessing a wedding entertainment. The bride and groom had places of honor, and the bride was quite as coy as the weeniest fairy or mortal bride ever was. The Scholastic mortal watched their antics and merry-making with the greatest wonder and admiration. The ease with which they moved around was wonderful to see. While some drank wine from enormous leaf cups, others tempted the women with tid-bits the size of a calf. Soon they appeared to have come to the end of their calfskins of wine, for they were squeezing out the last drops and looking about for more, and some were even sorely lamenting their miscalculation. The wine caves were in a remote region, where they were timid about going at night, because of the Dwarf Spirits, who set all sorts of traps for them.

Every hill and knoll is inhabited by them—every tree and flower; in fact, it is owing to the "little people" even in these days that the sign-boards are all turned wrong, to the confusion of tourists, and the consternation and dismay of lovers, who *lose their way*, are *detained*, kept from getting home early according to orders, and who have a hard time of it in many ways, thanks to the fairies' tricks.

Scholasticus thought it a pity that such jolly folk should have their pleasure spoiled for want of wine, and catching up a bottle of his own, threw it among them. In its flight it grew to be as large as a hogshead, and well-nigh frightened the giants out of their wits. But one who had observed the quarter from which the flask came went to the porch to discover the offender. On seeing Scholasticus, the Giant addressed him thus:

"Thou art a mortal! A human brother! We are the remnant of the first children of the earth. Our race is nearly extinct. As living creatures, to-night we pass away, yet do not entirely leave the earth, but take shape and dwell in the rocks and boulders, cliffs and mountains. We have never yet allowed a mortal to keep his eyes after having looked upon our gatherings; but as this is to be our last meeting, and as thou hast a good heart, and hast wished to prolong our cheer, thou art welcome to come among us without fear of harm."

Scholasticus accepted the Giant's invitation, and when he went among them they pledged him repeatedly in his own wine. The bride opened the dance with him for her partner. They were not very well matched as to size; but that seemed to make very little difference. A giant of her importance could not becomingly stoop to a mortal, so she took him up to *her* and and went round and round in the mazes of an intricate dance, until the poor scholar was *ready* to drop, but *could not*. On she went, quicker and quicker, neither noticing nor seeming to care whether he were on the ground or off it, until all of a sudden a great splash of water came down among them.

"A rain-drop!" cried the Giants as with one voice, and immediately fled. The mortal screamed "*The deluge!*" so loudly that he woke to find the Giants gone! Fire-flies, tents, mushrooms, and banquet! Fairies gone! Nothing left save the muskrat huts and the scholastic mortal, who found himself kicking about among them as if determined to leave no reminder of the night's doings.

Old Martha, the housekeeper, with an empty water-pail and a knowing eye, stood over him, and the scholar concluded, when he saw the numerous bottles lying around him, that he must have been pretty far gone in his cups.

But for many evenings afterward, when old Martha had gone to vespers, he sat in the porch, with a great quantity of wine to meet the demand, awaiting the return of the Giants; but they had said truly their last meeting had taken place, but they may be seen in the conical rocks and spires of the cliffs, standing sentinel to guard the home of the Great Spirit.

The muskrats no longer build their huts in the flat land below the Mission, but the meadow is still the greenest spot on the island to-day.

INDIAN RIP VAN WINKLE.

AT Gros Carp, near the Straits, Kandawagonosh lived with his parents; and as he was handy at bow-making and canoe-building, could make, set, or haul in the nets which provided them with fish from the lakes; had a clear eye, a steady hand, and unerring aim—his fleet foot reaching the side of the doe as soon as the arrow which sped from his bow. He was of much use to them, and they realized their loss when one day he went to take up the nets, and failed to return; and when his canoe was found crushed on the rocks, they mourned him as dead. They made a little house of bark—a thatched grave—and placed within it his best pipe, his bit of vermilion, a knife, a kettle, and some bows and arrows; together with his favorite dog, which they buried alive, in the belief that the creature would find his master wherever he was. In the bottom of the grave they placed the totem pole—a sort of certificate of character—in the hope that the wandering spirit would find and by it know the especial place assigned for its last sleep.

But the Spirit of Kandawagonosh did not return to look for its grave. He met and married, beneath the waves, the beautiful daughter of a powerful Water Spirit. Blissfully they lay upon the soothing waves, and enjoyed together the light touches of the mists of love. Time passed swiftly in the Emerald Land; love and happiness and a large family of laughing spirits made the centuries seem as but a few short weeks. At last he said: "My mother will be needing the firewood and pemmican, which I am in the habit of providing for her; my father wishes my help with the arrow-making and dressing of skins after his long hunt." And he prevailed upon his wife to allow him to leave her for a while, that he might go and comfort them.

"You are a good son," she said to him, "and should be a faithful husband." She put into his hand as she let him go a little box of birch bark ornamented with quills. "Keep this always in the bag at your belt. It must never be opened. If the box is opened, my spirit, which will go with you to guide and protect, will be driven away. Your wife, your children, and the Emerald Land will be lost to you forever."

The Spirit of Kandawagonosh returned to his once familiar village, to find his home and his parents gone, and in the place where they had dwelt was heaped a great mound of stones. As he passed in his lonely wanderings the desolate place selected for his grave, a peculiar sound attracted his attention; it was as though a dog were scratching and barking beneath the earth. He thought of his dear parents, and sighed that he had parted from them forever. He sat down on his grave to sorrow over the loved and lost, and thought that it would be a good thing to return to the Emerald Land. While thinking of his wife, but not of the penalty of his act, he lifted the lid of the precious box which Undinala had given him. A cry of despair escaped him as he saw a cloud of light blue vapor issue from it, in the shape of Undinala, and disappear in the distant ether.

In an instant he was changed from a stalwart youth to a decrepit old man; and in another the dog had worked his way out of the grave, where he had remained so long waiting to conduct his master to the Happy Hunting Grounds, and seizing him by the throat, dragged him beneath the earth, there to remain till the great Festival of the Dead should release him from the power of the angry dog, and permit him to enter the Fields of the After Life.

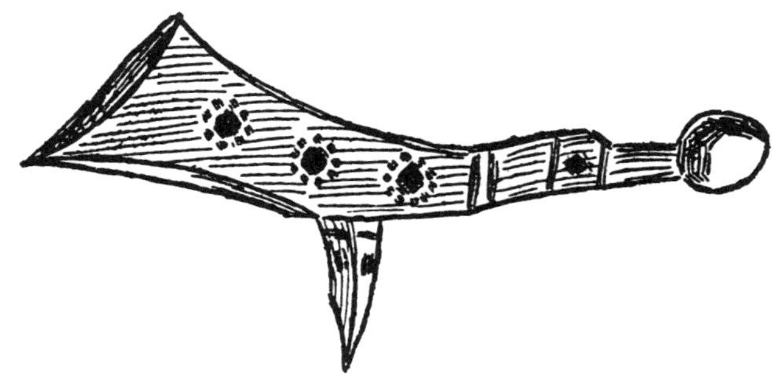

THE HEROISM OF KEWANOKO.

MARCH is often the coldest and most tedious month of the long winters of the "Lake Region." While the inhabitants of more southern climes are watching the bursting of the buds and the twittering of the birds in the faintly green branches of the trees, those of the isolated islands of the straits are enduring the rigors of northern winter.

The Ides of March was a fatal season to a once mighty emperor; and that the same season was not also fatal, hundreds of years later, to the young Indian, Wa-wa-tam, who was "mail-carrier" between the Island of Mackinac and the villages of the mainland, was not the fault of the weather, but due entirely to the heroism of Kewanoko, his betrothed bride.

In such a month of March, then, when the people of the Island Mission were hoping for an early "breaking up," because the crows had come, though far from expecting it, now that the wind had changed from south to north, and was hurling upon them the most cruel storm of the winter, our story opens, and in the cruelest of winter storms was the heroism of the Indian girl proved.

A white blanket of snow and sleet had covered the hills; miles away the lake steamed and smoked upon the borders of the ice-fields; the hedges, towering high above the rotting old palisade behind which they grew, were all buried deep beneath great frozen drifts, which had piled themselves about the Mission House, whose lower windows were heaped with it, doorways entirely hidden and useless, and entrance made by paths on the drift tops through the second-story windows.

Kewanoko lived at the Mission, where she was being taught the Christian religion, and to make letters and figures on the blackboard. She was very happy, and usually took great pains to learn the tasks which the good "Black Coat" set her; but to-day she could not do them, because her lover was out upon the ice in the fearful storm, and she dreaded the worst that could befall him. Over and over again she wiped from the tiny window-pane her frozen breath while painfully endeavoring to penetrate the blackness of the night, to catch, if possible, the first glimpse of the long-delayed courier whom she loved.

The child of aboriginal parents, whose death had found them in a night like this, what wonder if dark thoughts brood in her mind, and that, though a "Mission Christian," superstition and the storm should whisper of the direful fate which awaited Wa-wa-tam in the difficulties of his journey, which neither Christian God nor Indian Spirit could avert without some human aid.

The good Missionary urged her to take some rest, reminding her that she "must trust in her God, believing that what *is* is best in whatever case." But with the storm raging every moment in wilder and increasing fury, the ice cracking and booming with ear-splitting reverberations, and the night-wind moaning in her ears, how was it possible for her to have faith? How put her trust in an unseen God, who *could*, if he *would*, quell the storm, but who did not?

"A test of faith," the good man said.

The moon shone fitfully through great gust-driven clouds, adding pale terrors to the night; while out upon the frozen waters, Wa-wa-tam, "the bravest of brave braves," was being whipped to death by the icy lashes of the wind. In fancy she heard the distant baying of the dogs. Was it fancy, or did she truly hear their mournful cries? A ray of hope. She waited, listening. Surely she would soon behold him—the dogs would bring him home.

The dogs? In the slow dawning of the northern morning they drag their weary and dejected lengths to meet her welcoming hand, to lay themselves in coats of icy mail all trembling at her feet, their pitying looks reflecting all the tortured thought of her kindly eyes, to hang their heads in grief that they had not brought Wa-wa-tam to share with them her greeting as of yore.

The spark of hope trembled and died out. But, hold! From among the faithful herd she missed one more faithful than the rest; and hark! again and again, above the howling of the storm, she hears the freezing creature's cry. "God wills the best;" but it was not *best* that Wa-wa-tam should die, while she had strength and God's help to save him! Courage filled her heart. The combined strength of a hundred forest mothers lived again within the girlish frame at this supreme moment of her young life. She prayed for strength by which to prove the Christian's God a God of love and mercy, and to save her lover's life.

Springing to the sledge which hung beside the outer door, ready for the need of rich or poor alike, she threw the hempen harness upon the waiting dogs, flung wide the door, and leaping upon the simple *traine de glacé*, with a frenzied cry from the dogs, they tore away—away over walls of snow and ice which barred their progress. Away! away! to where the sun was rising in the east, though as yet unseen for clouds of whirling snow.

The wind moaned sadly through the bare branches of the maples by the porch, rattled each loose pane in the decayed window frames, sifted between the yawning cracks of the foundations and the crumbling mortar of the old stone chimneys of the Mission House as Kewanoko left its shelter to search amid the blinding storm for her lover. The snow fell in thick wet sheets upon her as she sped across the thundering, heaving ice bridge. Great flocks of crows flew before her, cawing of their hunger and cold—cawing of the naked forest which gave them no shelter. White gulls floated on storm-beaten wings over her head, and the girl shuddered at the thought of the dear flesh which soon might break their fast.

The wind rushed onward, and with it the weary dogs and their heroic mistress. Gusts of sleety rain cut into their flesh and stiffened their limbs until they were almost incapable of motion, but no thought of fatigue or weariness or turning entered the brave girl's mind. On and on they went, until the way was blocked at last, and the worn-out animals could go no farther. A ridge of broken and crushed ice, a mountain of bristling points thrown up by the storm-lashed water and frozen into an impassable barrier, rose before them.

The dogs gave up; with a moan of sorrow the faithful creatures laid down in their tracks, to rise no more. But hark! their moan of death is answered by a bark of welcome beyond the barrier. With renewed energy and a joyful cry at the sound, the girl sprang onward once again. The thousand Manitous of storm and pain and death had leagued against them, but the God of Love and Mercy would save her—would save *Wawatam* yet.

Sharp as razors and brittle as glass is the way she takes, but brave as love itself, and all undaunted by the monstrous difficulties before her, Kewanoko scrambled onward, upward, slipping, falling backward at each painful step, stumbling and lurching forward at each agonized effort, until at last she reached the glassy height which hid from her view that which she hoped yet dreaded to find.

The lodges and shanties of the fishermen, who each year thus perilously procured a meagre livelihood for themselves and families, lay before her, scattered far and wide by the winds; the frozen and brittle bodies of those who had occupied them flung in broken fragments upon the heaving covering of the turbulent waters. Merciful God! and must she search among the scattered remnants which but yesterday were men, for the brave youth to whom she had pledged her love and for whom she would gladly give her life?

"Everything has an end," even misery, and Kewanoko had come to the end of hers when, lying almost at her feet so near that she had overlooked them in the horror of the more distant scene, she saw Wawatam lying beside the bodies of his horse and dog, his head pillowed on the clumsy leathern mail bag which bore the seal of the Government who trusted him, asleep! *Almost* that last dreamless sleep which comes to all. *Almost* the frosty-fingered herdsman had claimed Wawatam for his own.

With a low whinny of welcome to the rescuers of its friend and master, the more tenderly nurtured animal breathed its last; but the dog, inured to the cold and hardship of northern winters, though weak from exposure and famished for food, staggered to its feet in frozen joy to lick the saving hand held out to him, then sank again beside the freezing form of his dear human friend to share with him the small warmth of its shaggy body.

The wind veered to the south with increased violence. The ice was fast breaking up outside the ridge of sharp bergs among which Wawatam lay. Too late? Had Kewanoko reached his side too late? She cried aloud in her grief, and the wind howled its answer over the frozen waters; "Too late! too late!"

The way was difficult, but she plunged

bravely toward the foot of the ridge, striving to reach her lover's side before his spirit departed, but her frozen limbs no longer obeyed her loving will. It seemed that the clear blue ice swayed beneath her, while mirrors of silver swung above and beyond, showing her lover now in this place, now in that, until bewildered she sunk upon her knees.

The wind kissed Wawatam and played over him, and at that kiss warm life diffused itself over his frame. Banished were his fears of death, his oppressed breathings and all his pain. Another and another kiss of the wind, and every vein streamed with living joy. Why fear, why grieve when life was so fair? The sound of the booming waves and the crashing ice fell on his ears like the discharge of artillery, mingled with the melodious chiming of great bells. The wind played about him, and he knew not if life or death possessed him, but felt himself to be rising and falling and swaying in a maze of warmth and beauty. The scenes of his simple forest life passed in minute review before his mind, while the waters were foaming beneath him, the snow fast covering him, and the dog still clinging to him.

Another kiss of the wind!

A cry of agony escaped him, and at that cry the brave girl who had come to save him, crept to his side. With a yelp of hope the dog left them, his chilled limbs gaining strength and warmth and more than usual fleetness with each bounding step that brought him nearer to the land and safety. The delighted barkings of the sagacious animal, when he came upon the dead bodies of the dogs who had accompanied their brave mistress in her attempt to rescue Wawatam, were changed to mournful whimperings when he found them helpless; but in spite of frozen eyelids and snow obstructed lashes, in spite of every discouragement which met him in the way, of broken ice and heavy snow, and no visible path, he forged onward for some distance, then —stopped still. He listened to the rumbling sound of the angry pent-up waters striving to free themselves! He advanced a little. Would he go on, or was he lost amid the confusion of the elements? No. He turns and sniffs his way again over the tracks he had made, and with almost human intelligence—more, an unerring animal instinct—returned to those dear friends whom he no longer dared to leave. His frantic effort to rouse the drowsy girl was assisted by a smart blow from the *traine de glacé*, which, loosened from its slight holdings in the slippery ledge where it had lodged when the dogs had freed themselves from thair harness, fell, striking her smartly on the cheek. She woke to the knowledge of the danger, which but for the timely help of her dumb friend, might never have been averted. Slowly divining what had happened, and the terrible fate which awaited them unless she acted quickly, she got up on her benumbed feet, and with a prayer to the God of Love and Mercy that he would not desert them—she had faith to believe that His divine strength could save them even now—she drew the sledge nearer the sleeping form of her lover whom she believed to be already dead, and by a mighty effort, somewhat assisted by the position of the body, managed to roll it down upon the narrow *traine*. After what seemed to her frozen senses hours of labor, she had bound him fast to the fragile conveyance, strapped herself with the mail wallet into the vacant place beside him, made a noose in the rope which was knotted upon the rolling front of the *traine* and slipped it over the head of the dog who waited to bear them to the land and safety.

Kewanoko could do no more. She must trust the dog for the rest.

Not a moment was lost by the powerful creature, who, trembling with fear and eager to be off, needed no order to advance—no "*marche a la maison*" of the courier to send him speeding homeward.

The sun peered through a mist of fine snow—the wind increasing in fury crushed and pounded the ice bridge over which they sped with terrific force. The heart of the half-frozen Kewanoko was filled with dread, and hope was almost dead within her, for she knew that the ice over which they sped could not long withstand the force of the gale. Behind them she could see the treacherous mass boiling and seething, as in a mighty cauldron, and before them, in the fast lessening distance, the narrow strait—the land and safety. Would the treacherous bridge hold until they reached it? A fearful report deafened her, and the ice parted at their very feet!

By making a detour they cleared the crack not a moment too soon, for in the moment of their retreat the place was open water, with the ice crushing and jamming and swirling before the force of the wind which carried it to the "big waters" of Lake Huron. Each moment was a lifetime!

The dog, uttering terrified cries, leaped from ice cake to ice cake, drawing the *traine* with its precious human freight behind him, and which by a magnificent effort of strength Kewanoko kept right side up, as it half floated, half slid over the upheaving mass until at last they reached the firm ice of the harbor, and soon after the shelter of the Mission.

"They have robbed me of my children," wailed the dying Wind, while the storm, robbed of its prey, beat upon them in a last effort to destroy.

"A God of Love and Mercy, mighty to save!" sighed the girl as she closed her eyes.

"Sleep, and not death, hath kissed them," murmured the man of God as the lovers opened their eyes to the light and warmth of the log fire of the Mission Kitchen, before which rested the dog.

WARDS OF THE GOVERNMENT.

SEVEN YEARS' TIDE.

IT was the custom among the Northern Indians to prove the courage and strength of their young men by various tests, and none but those who endured them unflinchingly, or accomplished them successfully, were allowed manly privileges, or chosen as warriors.

Wolf's Head, a chief, had three sons, whom he wished to have named as warriors and given the right to sit in the councils. These sons were ready to undergo the manhood tests, and begged to be put to the performance of them as promptly as possible.

The two eldest got through with their painful and hazardous tasks with credit, and were at once given place among the band of braves who were preparing for the warpath; but Singing Sands, the youngest of the three, having been the most urgent to have his task allotted him, because of his persistency, was given the most arduous and difficult of any yet devised or undertaken by the men of their tribe. This was a seven years' test. If successful, he was to be made a chief—the right of inheritance to his descendants.

The seven years' test was to be a journey on foot around the chain of great lakes. The conditions allowed one year for the tramp along the shore of each. He was to secure treasure of a portable nature to present to his people on his return, as a sign of his good will. He would be allowed to retain one-third of the property he should accumulate for the maintenance of his family. On reaching the Atlantic, he must wait upon its shore to witness the *mingling* of the waters, which took place before the turning of the tides.

From Lake Superior he was to bring silver and copper, out of which to make kettles and articles of adornment. Wampum beads he was to gather upon the beaches of Lake Michigan. Fish and game, preserved in the salt of the Saginaw, were to be taken from Lake Huron; war feathers from the marshes of St. Clair—the moulting ground of northern birds; fruits from Lake Erie and its islands; and fine furs and skins of great animals from the forest borders of Lake Ontario. These treasures, together with a *wife*, he was to bring back with him, if his quest failed not.

"At the big salt water, where the Seven Tides meet, thou shalt find the woman whom the Master of Life hath named thy wife," said old Wolf Head. "Her Spirit will go before thee in all thy journeyings in the shape of a Red Swan. Though blind—until thy coming shall give light to her eyes—she will elude thee, yet lead thee; but be not discouraged shouldst thou not overtake the Red Swan—called Lonely Bird—until all thy task is done. If thou art successful, the Swan will not refuse thee."

Singing Sands was of a domestic nature; his soul yearned not for the paint and spoils of war, but rather for home joys and ties; and it pleased him well that his father should tell him these things.

"At the turning of the Seven Waters, find thy mate," said the medicine men. "Hasten, that the Lonely Bird need no longer mourn for the mate with whom she hopes to enter the Fields of Plenty."

Singing Sands was willing to become the husband of the Red Swan, who had been so long a prisoner at the *edge* of the tides, but determined to accomplish his task, if for no other reason than to effect her release. He vowed that, in spite of all obstacles, he would win the wealth demanded by the prophets, the confidence of his people, and Lonely Bird besides.

The journey from the northern home of Singing Sands was a hard one. The paths he traversed were frozen, and so rough that the music of his steps was slow and disconnected, though never discordant; the rhythm broken and sad, though never complaining—for Singing Sands was a youth of good heart and noble thoughts; fault-finding and discontent were not among his characteristics; he made the best of every ill. So when the ragged rocks tore his fine rabbit-skin moccasins and blistered his feet, he uttered no sigh, but trudged bravely along until he came to the Big Brother of the Sea (Lake Superior), which he found to be covered with clear blue ice. Some buzzards flew over his head; he shot two and boiled them well, so that the flesh fell easily from their bones, and soon had a pair of swift runners for his feet, made of the sharp, well-scraped and polished backs of the birds. They bore him painlessly, and with the speed of the wind, across the ice to the narrow Sault along whose banks were set the lodges of strage tribes.

These people were most friendly to him, and he remained for a time among them, questioning as to their knowledge of the tides, studying the heavens, and learning what he could about the great Lakes, whom these Indians worshiped as gods, and who informed him that the wonderful upward-streaming lights of silver and rose color which covered the sky at night were always brightest when the tides were about to turn. These lights, his friends informed him, were more brilliant than usual at the present time; and it was looked on as a good omen for him as the cone-shaped lights were shining in groups of *seven*, to show that the rivalry between the East and West Winds had ended in the victory of the West Wind, which would prevail for *seven* years.

Singing Sands was glad of this because the greater part of his journey lay in the direction of the Big Salt Water, and the West Wind was favorable. As the tides had already turned toward the sea he bade his friends good-bye and hastened away to reach the Atlantic before the meeting of the waters should take place. His friends had endeavored to discourage him as to the result of his task, as the Big Salt Water always resisted the attempts made by the Brother Lakes to unite with it, and declared it to be an undertaking altogether impossible.

They were aware that the Red Swan

mourned for a mate, but did not believe that she would ever be released to join hands with any man.

The Saulteurs were a wise people, their prophets considered infallible, and Singing Sands started on his way in spite of warnings of failure and predictions of disaster; but as he was possessed of no unearthly or magical powers—unless a dauntless courage and strong frame could be called such—he needed all his resolution, his cheerfulness under difficulties, and his strength of purpose to take him successfully through the next five years.

When in his travels he chanced upon a vacated fireplace, he soon made out whether the people who had made it were warriors or hunters, by the shape and disposition of the tent-poles. If hunters, he joined them for a few days to find out the nearest way to the coast; if warriors, he avoided them if possible. One day a flock of screaming birds led him to a high cliff, from which he could see the sort of warfare his brothers were engaged in, and at this place a black witch, disguised as a *cat*, tempted him to join with his brothers and win his honors easily.

The handful of valiant braves whom his brothers and the young men with them had entrapped in a complete circle of fire, were all that was left of the goodly band which had been fighting for days against great odds. Their escape was impossible, and each attempt was met by enemies, more cruel and vindictive than the flames, who yelled and leaped with frantic triumph as the war club and the tomahawk did their fearful work.

It was soon over. The flames crept nearer and nearer the beleagured ones, for whom there was no refuge nor escape; the crags behind them were white with heat, and no man could scale them; the lake spread out its cool blanket so near that the red flames were reflected in it; but no man dared pass the blazing ring and the thousand poisoned arrows outside it to reach the cooling comfort which it offered. They knew that they must die. They sang the death song in unison, covered their heads with their blankets, and were still.

Singing Sands had never looked upon such a scene, and had not thought that his brothers could be guilty of such cruelties. Their shouts of victory filled him with shame, which was increased by the black cat leaping upon his shoulder to whisper of the "glory to be had by stripping the scalps from the heads of the vanquished dead."

He flung the creature from him, ashamed at the thought; and, when spitting and scratching in fearful rage the cat disappeared in a blue flame, he knew that he had been tempted by an evil spirit to do an evil deed. He turned from the scene, as the ravenous birds settled down upon the bodies of the slain; but he never forgot the horrible picture nor the part his brothers had in it. He was comforted by the thought that the cat had not been able to tempt him, and that "*if his quest failed not*," he would allow no such practices among the people whom he should govern.

Lest his heart become too heavy with these thoughts, his guardian spirit, who followed him in the sky, gave him an occasional glimpse of the Red Swan, who often dropped a shell for his wampum chain, or gave him a feather for his war-lock or the more ceremonial head-dress which he would be required to wear when he became a chief.

His first year's tramp around Lake Superior ended with a second visit to the Sault. Leaving there he made the *détour* and passed the Sacred Island of the Straits, remained for a time among the Beavers to investigate their system of bridge making, invaded the country of the Chi-ca-gous and took from their malarial marshes the seed of the leek and the wild onion, which the medicine men informed him was a cure for the shaking fevers which sometimes assailed the people. He circled the shores of Mich-i-saw-gye-gan, and once more came upon the sands of the Sacred Island, where he delayed for the rest and refreshment he so much needed, and to invoke the protection and guidance of the Spirit of the Great Turtle who dwelt in its subterranean caves.

After resting upon the cool terraces and refreshing himself upon the sunlit hills, Singing Sands entered the enchanted paths of the underground abode of the wise men, who came forth to instruct their visitor in the use of herbs and magic.

The third year gave him the fish and game

of Ka-to-gie (Lake Huron), which, when preserved in the salt of the Sag-e-na's, promised great comfort in the way of food; while from the great "White Rock" of its bay of Thunder he obtained many arrow-heads, which were sure to be highly prized by his people.

At the beginning of the fourth year he reached Ot-sie-ki-tah's (Lake St. Clair) clear waters, and coursed the smaller water-ways, where he gathered the war feathers demanded by the prophets. He found this a most difficult thing to do, as the ice had so dammed up the stream that Ot-sie-ki-tah and even the wide strait of Waw-we-au-to-nong (Detroit) were drained, and the birds gone to other haunts for the winter.

The fifth year saw him the possessor of even greater fortune. Grains of various description, sweet mondamin, and fruits from the islands of Erigas (Lake Erie) were laid at his feet by the friendly people who dwelt there, and who gave him wine and taught him its use and manufacture. Singing Sands felt that he had done well in placing himself under the protection of the Spirit of the Great Turtle, since all things had prospered with him since that act of faith and humility.

Over the precipitous sides of the great walled cataract he clambered in safety, and at the end of the sixth year, during which he had taken much game and secured valuable furs and skins to add to his stores, the worst of the test of his manly qualities was over. But never for a single moment of all the fatiguing years had the thought of failure entered his mind, and never had he given up the hope of winning the Red Swan for his bride. By her guidance he had reached the Big Sea water, and he believed that his reward was near. The ocean was untroubled and everything seemed propitious for a comfortable seventh year.

He believed he could satisfy the wise men and prophets that he had honorably fulfilled the conditions of his task. He would share with them the products of his seven years' toil, and when the spell of enchantment under which Lonely Bird had lived so long was lifted and she was once more a woman, he would claim his reward.

So eager was Singing Sands now to finish his task that he *ran* down the wide beaches and over the rocky shores of the Atlantic with greater speed than ever; his singing mingled with the wild tones of the Sea until Florida, the land of flowers and everlasting youth, was reached. Then, and not till then, did he take rest. His fatigue was very great, but his task was done, and the knowledge that before another moon had waned he would have a wife to cheer him, made him very happy.

Weariness overcame him and he threw himself down upon the ground to sleep. Great balls of *living* fire came and danced before his eyes so that he dared not close them. A voice told him that these flames were named "love" and "beauty" and "virtue" and "power," and that he must make them his own before he could possess the Lonely Bird. He sprang to catch them, but like will-o'-wisps they eluded him, now here, now there, until he fell to the earth exhausted and unsuccessful. The shade of the palm trees beneath which he lay soothed his tired brain and cooled his burning eyes, though the heavy lids could not remain closed while the balls of flame danced and played so near. Suddenly the balls came together and took the shape of a lovely woman, such as he had always dreamed his soul's mate would be.

At the sight of the lovely being moving slowly along the edge of the unruffled Sea, now and again beckoning him to follow, his energies were fired anew, and he determined to possess her or die in the attempt. His fatigue was great, his desire was greater! He sprang toward her—she was behind him! Her breath was upon his cheek—he turned to clasp her—she was gone! Vain was the elusive search; she had vanished! The winds fluttered the leaves and whispered of her sweet presence, but she was gone and he could not find her. The vision which had risen like a star to cheer his heart had suddenly set, leaving him once more lonely and desolate. He believed that in the spirit woman he had seen Lonely Bird as she would be in life, and loved her already. By her guidance he had come to the "Beautiful Land," and he determined to wait where he was until the Spirit should tell him what to do.

He set up his lodge, kindled a small fire on some stones near to show his friendly intentions, as was the custom of the people of the

North, and made himself a bed of grey moss on which to rest while awaiting orders.

An aged man—one of the never-to-be-vanquished Seminoles—looked in upon him as he lay stretched upon his newly-made couch to give him welcome to the Everglades, and to invite him to drink freely of the waters of a magical spring which ran near his door, that he might live forever. Four white feathers he gave him to fasten upon his tent poles, to signify that the occupant desired the protection of the spirits who dwelt at the Four Corners of the Earth; and four more he placed beneath the fire stones, to insure its burning forever. Brightly burning fires indicated that the householder was hospitably inclined. When he had placed pemmican and pounded maize about the tent poles with pipes and smoking material for the poor, the old man left him to his much-needed rest.

A long sleep and bath from the life-giving spring restored his strength and refreshed his mind; and to signify his willingness to further submit to the rulings of the Spirit of his guardian Shape, he returned to his lodge to begin a seven days' fast. His powers of endurance were as great as his faith, but he hoped to *subdue* his spirit by weakening his body, and by clearing his eyes and ears of disturbing sights and sounds, the sooner to witness the turning of the tides. His prayer was that his heart might be purified by the self-imposed penance, as his body had been invigorated by his toil, until he should be worthy of his chosen mate.

Seven days Singing Sands fasted and let the Spirit have its way with him. He was gifted with a fine ear and a sharp eye; his fasting did not lessen these qualities, and when, at the end of the seventh day, Lonely Bird fluttered toward him from the edge of the Sea, his quick ear immediately detected the familiar sound, and he went forth to meet her.

Often had Lonely Bird been cheered by the sound of Singing Sands' music as she led him toward the goal of his manly hopes, and loved the singer with all her heart; and as each day brought them nearer each other, her own plaintive song became less mournful and took a happier tone. The prayers of her lover and their pure echoings had unclosed the door of her imprisoned soul, and the wings which had beaten the darkness so long now bore her freely toward the mate who had come to give light to her eyes and make her life perfect.

With a great joy in his heart, the expectant lover left his lodge; and following the sound of the Swan's fluttering wings, was led to the edge of the Sea—to which she had modestly withdrawn at his approach. He called to her with words of encouragement and cheer; he murmured words of love, whose meaning, as it dawned upon her mind, so swelled her heart with love that the bonds which held her were broken, and the Red Swan was no longer a Lonely Bird. Her garments of feathers fell from her, and Singing Sands saw before him the lovely maiden who had eluded him when he had endeavored to make her his own before the appointed time.

As he folded her in his arms for the first time, having earned the right to hold her as his wife, the sun smilingly went over the edge of the Sea, and the Seven Tides blushed a rosy red as they turned, under the direction of the East Wind—to whom the Spirit had restored its previous power—and joined to bear the happy pair upon the streams which now flowed in the direction of the home which Singing Sands had left so long ago, and where his old father still watched and prayed for his return, that the starving people might be provided for.

The young couple were received with great rejoicings, and when the provisions were brought into camp and distributed among the people, Singing Sands was made Chief by acclamation. The waves and the winds, clouds, fish, birds, trees, herbs, flowers, leaves, and rocks, the earth and the air, and every living thing, were under his dominion, so great was his knowledge, and his fame as a medicine man and prophet went out among all the nations.

The Swan, no longer doomed to grope in darkness, grew more lovely with each passing day, and proved herself a worthy mate for so great a chief. Peace dwelt in the lodges, and there were no wars among those whom Singing Sands governed.

Sons were born to Singing Sands; and when they were old enough, the mother taught them the beauty of obedience, the dignity of courage, the necessity for perseverance and cheerful endurance; and when they were men they had the same hopes and performed the same task which their father had accomplished in his youth.

Every seventh year the Big Salt Water receives the waters of the Brother Lakes, to send them back upon returning tides with health to the people and wealth to the land.

[NOTE.—Considerable doubt exists as to the cause of the periodic rise and fall of the Great Lakes, but the fact that they do rise and fall remains.

We find a memorandum of the fact of a seven years' tide in the Journal of Captain Morris, of Her Majesty's Eighteenth Infantry, 1764:

"That the waters of the Great Lakes rise for seven years and fall for seven years; in fact, there is a seven years' tide. General Bradstreet, while encamped on the shores of Lake Erie, lost a great many boats and large quantities of provisions and baggage by the *sudden rise* of the water, no wind being perceptible."]